TOULOUSE-LAUTREC

B
TOU
LOUSE-
LAUTREC

Horwitz, Sylvia L.

Toulouse-Lautrec:
his world

DATE			
APR 13 '77			
MAY 19 '77			
MAY 31 '77			
MAR 3 '80			
APR 11, '80			
Jan			
MAY 04 '81			
MAY 27 '81			
DEC 1 3 '83			
MAR 1 3 '84			
FE 17 '85			

Toulouse-Lautrec: His World

Toulouse-Lautrec: His World

by Sylvia L. Horwitz

With photographs
of the artist and his work

2789

Harper & Row, Publishers
New York, Evanston, San Francisco, London

The author wishes to thank the publishers for permission to quote from *The Unpublished Correspondence of Henri de Toulouse-Lautrec,* edited by Lucien Goldschmidt and Herbert Schimmel, published by Phaidon Press, Ltd., London, and Frederick A. Praeger, Inc., New York.

Frontispiece: photograph of Toulouse-Lautrec, 1896.
(From H. Roger Viollet, Paris)

For my brother Erwin

Contents

Author's Note

I am grateful to the Countess Attems, nee Marie Tapié de Céleyran, for the many insights I gained into the character of Toulouse-Lautrec through the letters and family reminiscences contained in her book, *Notre Oncle Lautrec* (Geneva, Switzerland: Pierre Cailler, 1963).

I am indebted also to P. Huisman and M. G. Dortu, whose *Lautrec par Lautrec* presents an admirable portrait of the painter, and to the memoirs of those contemporaries who knew and admired him, including François Gauzi, Maurice Joyant, Pierre Mac Orlan, and Thadée Natanson.

Finally, my warm thanks to Stella and Leonard Seidenman, for allowing me free use of their fine collection of Toulouse-Lautrec lithographs, posters, books, and other material.

1

THE TWENTY-FOURTH of November, 1864, was the longest
day anyone in Albi could remember. The rain never
seemed to let up. Hour after hour the storm kept crashing through the hills, seeming to grow in intensity, and
still there was no news from the big house. Between the
thunder and the suspense, the people of Albi—who were
a superstitious lot anyway—were on edge.

The little town in the Midi (the South of France)
should have been asleep long before. Instead, candles
still flickered through shuttered windows, like poor re-
lations of the blaze of lights on the hill. From time to
time someone put his head out the window and looked
up at the ramparts. The great house flanking the cathe-
dral looked almost supernatural against the lightning-
streaked sky. The townsfolk could imagine Count
Alphonse pacing the mansion's length, waiting for the
birth of his first child.

Suitably, it was a boy. His name was almost as long as he was: Henri Marie Raymond de Toulouse-Lautrec Monfa. His lineage, as every schoolboy in Albi knew, was even longer. For a thousand years and more, the warriors, Crusaders, noblemen, and princes who bore his name had dominated the countryside from their high place on the hill.

Albi loved to talk about the Toulouse-Lautrecs. Their comings and goings enlivened many a dull winter evening. Old-timers swapped stories about the newborn's grandfather, who could still bag more pheasants in a day's shooting than any of his sons. "The Black Prince," they called him, because of his coal-black beard and stern bearing, his piercing eyes, his fearful temper. When *le Prince Noir* came to Albi from his country estate, people kept out of his way.

The baby's father, on the other hand, was a colorful, unredeemed eccentric. The good housewives of Albi never tired of wondering what Count Alphonse would be doing next. One minute he was washing out his socks in the river Tarn and the next he was galloping off to the hunt in some outlandish costume.

Nobody had ever expected the hot-blooded Alphonse to settle down to family life. The women still talked about his sumptuous wedding a year ago. The men took bets on how long he would be a faithful husband. Nevertheless, when he surprised everybody by marrying his own first cousin, the practical folk of Albi began counting vineyards and castles on their fingers. Countess Adèle

Tapié de Céleyran, gentle and unassuming though she was, would never end up in the poorhouse. By joining her fortune to his own, Count Alphonse had made this tiny infant the heir to some of the most princely holdings in the Midi.

Tradesmen and farmers rolled up their sleeves to prepare for the baptismal feasting. The "Toulouse stomach" was famous for miles around. The amount of food prepared in the big kitchens on the hill could have stocked half the larders in town. Family and guests came from all over the Midi to feast on deer and pheasant, salmon and trout, jellied eel, pâté de foie gras, and rare cheeses from as far away as Paris. It took one solid week of celebration to establish beyond doubt that Henri de Toulouse-Lautrec was born.

The storm was over. Life in Albi was back to normal. Now that his heir had arrived, Count Alphonse was impatient to be off again. Galloping back to his stables and hunting dogs at the Château du Bosc, some thirty miles from Albi, he left his wife and week-old son to follow him in the horse-drawn carriage.

It was a jolting, bumpy ride at best. The rocks washed down from the hills by the storm made the going rougher than usual. Countess Adèle, exhausted from the birth and the revelry, held Henri tightly in her arms and braced herself against the back seat of the carriage.

As the horses turned a narrow bend in the road she caught a glimpse in the distance of the Château du Bosc, where the Black Prince reigned like a feudal lord. Its rough, almost military walls dominated the surroundings as they had for centuries. Even this far away she could make out the moat. The turrets stood out above the walls like sentinels.

Countess Adèle loved the Château du Bosc as much as her husband did. As a small girl growing up she had often played in the cobblestoned courtyard when she came to visit her cousins. The whole third floor of the château had belonged to the children—their own privileged, protected world. She remembered the picnics on the river below, the games of badminton and croquet on the lawn, the Sunday teas; the enormous banquets, attended to by an army of servants, to toast somebody's birthday with sparkling wine in crystal goblets.

The coachman slowed the horses to a walk. As they drove over what had once been the drawbridge and through the massive iron gate, Countess Adèle was struck by how little the Château du Bosc seemed to change with the years. The passage of time and the world outside had remarkably little effect on her father-in-law and his domain. The Black Prince still lived in medieval splendor with his daughter and three sons, their wives and their children, their servants and their grooms, their horses, dogs, cormorants, and falcons.

Ensconced in this castle, Henri grew up to the touch of silk and velvet, the gleam of silver and fine porcelain, the clap of a hand and the stamp of a foot. It didn't take him long to discover his place among a horde of doting relatives and retainers.

The Château du Bosc as it looks today.

He was a handsome child with a bright and happy nature. His grandmother called him *le petit bijou*, "the little jewel." "Henri sings from morning till night," she wrote. "He's like a cricket that cheers up the whole house. When he's away we feel a great emptiness, because he fills the place of twenty people."

No matter how many cousins shared the third floor of the château, Henri was the *Général en Chef* of the nursery. When he wasn't producing puppet shows, he was inciting minor rebellions in chapel or leading gallops through the corridors, making frontal attacks on the pantry or undermining authority through pure charm and guile. He would have been even more spoiled than he was if his mother hadn't tried her best, with the help of his tutor Abbé Peyre, to discipline and instruct him.

It wasn't easy, but he was an excellent student and began learning his letters when he was three. A lisp didn't prevent him from making demands in fluent French, interspersed with Midi dialect picked up from the servants. He was studying English, then Latin and Greek, before he was seven. But he was like quicksilver, never still. "A ball," his mother called him, bouncing from one enthusiasm to another, sampling all the joys that life at the château offered. Especially horses.

Count Alphonse liked to say that in his family a baby was baptized and then went right into the saddle. It was almost literally true. The first noises Henri could identify were the neighing of horses and the barking of dogs;

the first smell, the warm aroma of horses' bodies in the stable.

Almost as soon as Henri could walk, Pierre Grèzes, the groom, began teaching him to ride. When he sat astride a horse like a seasoned cavalier, the whole family and all the servants gathered around to exclaim. Even his usually unsmiling grandfather melted.

The Black Prince and his three sons were all great hunters. Life at the Château du Bosc resounded to the sound of the horn. Each dawn, after a gigantic breakfast, the men assembled in the courtyard. Count Alphonse and his brothers Charles and Odon, their guests, the grooms, the whippers-in (whose job was to keep the hounds from straying), the servants, the horses, the dogs —and the boy at the window upstairs—all waited tensely for the signal to start. It was a pageant that renewed its magic day after day. The pack bayed. The horses pawed the air with impatience. Henri held his breath. And then, imperious on his pure-blooded mount Usurper, the Black Prince would raise a gloved hand and slash the air with his hunting whip. They were off!

When he could no longer hear the clatter of hooves, Henri sneaked off to the stables—strictly out-of-bounds. He went from horse to horse, calling each by name and checking on the contents of the feed bags. Then he made for the kennels, where the dogs too old to hunt or wounded in yesterday's adventures were waiting for him. He sampled the warm dark bread, freshly baked for the pack, and inspected every animal. He finally went

9

back to Abbé Peyre and his lessons, but only until the next opportunity to escape—this time perhaps to the kitchens, where he would dip a small finger into the sauces with Toulouse-Lautrec expertise and give gastronomic advice to the cooks. The daytime hours flew by.

Evenings at the château were wonderful. Back from the hunt and famished, the men would sit down to a prodigal table and describe the day's adventures. After dinner the whole family sat together in the big drawing room for a quiet hour or two before bedtime. While the women worked at their embroidery or knitting, the men took pencils or modeling clay in hand to reproduce what they most loved: horses, hunting scenes, dogs, the people and life at the château.

Sprawled on his stomach, Henri drew pictures of his own. Blank pages came to life under his eager pencil, or the charcoal fragment he took from the fireplace: his father on a horse; his mother in the lamplight; a caricature of Abbé Peyre; mostly horses, dogs, animals, birds. Nobody was particularly surprised. Even the Black Prince liked to draw.

Henri's grandmother once laughingly said of her three sons that they derived "three pleasures from the death of a woodcock—the sound of the gun, the sound of the fork, and that of the drawing pencil." Uncle Charles was especially gifted, and his nephew watched with delight as horse-drawn carriages and familiar faces flowed from pencil to sketch pad.

He was only four at the baptism of a new cousin, but

he saw no reason why he shouldn't sign the guest book along with the rest of the family. When told, "But you don't know how to write," he answered without hesitation, "It doesn't matter. I'll draw a steer." As though drawing were as natural as breathing.

There was never any question of what Henri would be when he grew up. The future heir to the Château du Bosc was born to be a gentleman. Already he rode horses, bred falcons, and raised cormorants. He imitated his father's walk and the way he sat a horse, ordered people about, tackled a roasted suckling pig. No one could doubt that the two of them sprang from the same roots.

But though Count Alphonse loved his son very much and was as impatient as Henri for the day they would go hunting together, he was not, as the townsfolk of Albi had suspected, a homebody. Even before Countess Adèle gave birth to their second son Richard, when Henri was not yet three, Count Alphonse had begun to spend more and more time away from home. If he wasn't at his hunting lodge at Loury, he was off to the races in Paris.

Most of the time his wife had no idea where he was. Occasionally he wrote her letters, usually about horses and dogs. Sometimes he dropped in unexpectedly— whether for a few days, a few weeks, or months, she never knew.

When Alphonse was in residence, life was full of the unexpected. Henri was enraptured at the sight of his glamorous father dressed in a Scottish kilt and brandishing a Japanese sword. Adèle was less enthralled to find her husband cooking Welsh rarebit in the fireplace of the big salon. His comings and goings were like explosions.

Any hopes Countess Adèle might have had that two sons would make a family man of their father were shattered when Richard died, within a year of his birth. She was left with an only son and a husband who was a visitor, familiar but erratic. The only bond between them was Henri. Before Henri had had time to grow jealous of his baby brother, he became his mother's sole interest in life.

She would have found all the happiness she could hope for in her son, but for one thing. She was worried about his health. His appetite was impressive even by Toulouse standards. Most of the time he lived out-of-doors in the warm Midi sun. And yet his bone structure was small and frail, his legs spindly.

The family had a habit of measuring all the children from time to time against one of the walls of a corridor in the château. Whenever it was his turn, Henri would stand up as straight as he could, almost on tiptoe, holding his head high, but the line marked with his name climbed imperceptibly. Cousins much younger than he soon towered over him. He didn't seem to grow.

2

WHEN HENRI WAS eight years old, the family moved to Paris. Countess Adèle hoped that a change of scenery (and the proximity of the races at Longchamps) might improve her marriage; and in any case, it was time for Henri to have more formal schooling than either she or Abbé Peyre could provide.

For Henri it was a sad day when the family's traveling coach, drawn by four gray post-horses, pulled up in front of the château. It was hard to leave his warm and protective world.

By 1872 the capital of France was already a city nearing two million in population. Whole families often crowded into quarters smaller than those occupied by the horses back home. Henri's first impression was of an enormous human beehive.

After the serenity of the château, with its muffled

sounds of woods and farm, the city was very noisy. The *clop-clop* of horses' hooves over rough cobblestones was deafening during rush hours, when the horse-drawn omnibuses were bringing workers to their jobs or home to their cheese and wine. The cries of the vendors selling fruits and vegetables, the song of the organ-grinder coaxing his monkey to dance, the chant of the knife sharpener, were very different from the sounds he was used to.

This tempo, this beat of a city, the throb of its crowds, were heady stuff to a boy born in Albi and raised in the sleepy Midi. Recovering from his homesickness, he began to thrive on the excitement.

It seemed to Henri that nobody stayed at home in Paris on a fine Sunday afternoon. The whole city put on its best clothes and took to the boulevards. Children rolled their hoops in and out of the crowds. Their parents ambled along exchanging gossip about their favorite music-hall idols or the latest government scandal. Everybody stopped to read the posters. There was hardly a wall, fence, or kiosk that didn't tell the wonders of the newest patent medicine or cigarette paper, the most up-to-date corset or apéritif.

Every so often one of the new rubber-tired bicycles went speeding down the avenue, startling the Sunday strollers. Its rider passed up the old wooden-wheeled contraptions (the Parisians called them "bone shakers") with insolent ease. The bewildered farmers who had brought their wares to the city's street markets weren't the only ones who asked themselves, "What next?" Everyone sensed that big changes were on the way.

The first time his parents took Henri to see the Champs Elysées by night, the broad boulevard was still illuminated by candles. Shadows played hide-and-seek with the faces around dimly lighted tables in restaurants. And then, almost before the boy had time to absorb Paris by candlelight, the oil lamp arrived. Soon after came the gas lamp to cast its soft radiance, like the afterglow of a sunset, over boulevards, squares, and theaters. The day was near when the incandescent electric bulb would cause all the world to call Paris *la Ville Lumière*, "the City of Light."

The Toulouse-Lautrecs installed themselves with accustomed comfort and luxury in a town house just off the Faubourg Saint-Honoré. It was not far from Henri's school and close by the fashionable shops on the rue Royale. Their cook had once presided over Queen Victoria's kitchens. Countess Adèle engaged an Irish governess with the improbable name of Miss Brain. Henri went to school in a Norwegian trap drawn by a pony. And Count Alphonse, got up like an English dandy, went riding every day in the Bois de Boulogne. He belonged to the exclusive Jockey Club, one of the last bastions of the nobility. During the racing season he divided his time between the tracks of Longchamps and Chantilly, sometimes taking his family with him, to Henri's great joy.

Sundays often found father and son either at the Botanical Gardens or at the zoo, observing and sketching the animals and birds they both loved so much. Alphonse's feeling for animals was genuine and deep. Through his father's eyes Henri came to see not "horses," but *a horse*, this particular horse, different from all other horses—as each person is different from all others. He always saw them in motion, quivering with life.

"Alphonse has undertaken his son's education in horsemanship," Adèle wrote home, "and he takes the child once a day to the Duphot stables. I hope that riding will be useful for his physical development and make him more robust. Also, I hope it will help Henri because he loves it more than any other member of the family. But he grows so slowly. . . ."

"*Le p'tit bonhomme*," the other boys called him at the Lycée Fontane: "the little fellow." But Henri didn't mind the nickname. He already had two best friends to whom neither his size nor his lisp mattered. When Henri thought up some new devilment with which to plague his teachers, he could count on his cousin Louis Pascal and Maurice Joyant not to reveal the source. In addition to enjoying each other's company during and after class, the three were friendly rivals in the classroom and shared most of the honors for top grades in French grammar, Latin, and Greek.

Countess Adèle was proud. "Although he's the youngest in the class," she reported to her mother, "his achievement is fourth in a group of forty boys"; and this in spite of frequent absences from school because of doctors' orders.

He began studying German. In English, the language

of gentlemen and jockeys, he was first in his class. But though he could speak in several languages, the boy's surest means of communication was the drawing pencil. He filled the margins of his Latin dictionary and French grammar with drawings: sketches of his schoolmates, caricatures of his teachers, the goings-on at school; and, of course, horses.

The first "real" painter that Henri knew was René Princeteau, a friend of his father's. Count Alphonse went regularly to Princeteau's studio and took his son with him. It was the boy's first glimpse into that color-streaked world of art to which he was already so attracted.

Monsieur Princeteau lived in a sort of artists' colony at the other end of the Faubourg Saint-Honoré, a part of Paris that was still more like country than city. Cluttered studios were strung along both sides of a narrow dead-end street. On a warm sunny day the artists kept their doors wide open in friendly coexistence. Easels propped to get maximum sunlight, they chatted while they worked, stopping occasionally to have a look at a neighbor's canvas or discuss a problem of perspective, borrow a tube of paint or drink a glass of wine. Their easy informality was contagious. Only among the grooms and trainers in the stables back home had Henri felt this warm camaraderie, this intimate atmosphere of shared interest.

Princeteau himself was very elegant: tall, frock-coated, top-hatted. Although his speech was guttural, it was hard to believe that he was born deaf, so skillfully had he learned to read lips and to speak. At thirty he was already an artist of some renown, and an expert horseman who loved and understood the animals he painted. While his father set up an easel at one side of the painter, Henri stood on a chair at the other side, observing, imitating. From time to time Princeteau would stop his own work to look over the boy's sketches, praising a bird in flight, gravely correcting the leg muscles of a horse. Henri glowed with pride.

Tuberculosis? Rickets? The doctors taking care of Henri had no way of determining exactly what was wrong; unfortunately, it would be another twenty years before the discovery of the X ray. They all agreed, however, that his bones were not growing properly. On their advice Countess Adèle decided to take her son back to the warmer climate and easier life of the Château du Bosc.

Henri was not too sad at having to interrupt his formal schooling a few months after his eleventh birthday. He received a tumultuous welcome from all the cousins he had left behind at the château and the many new ones recently arrived. (The marriage of Count Alphonse's sister to Countess Adèle's brother would alone contribute fourteen children to the clan.) Exuberantly, he resumed his place at the head of his troop, and proceeded once again to divide his time between his tutors, his frequent trips to health resorts for "the cure," and his new mania for collecting miniature toy carriages.

He was decidedly spoiled. Still, his mother saw to it that he kept up his studies. She herself supervised his English lessons. Uncle Charles taught him how to do watercolors. The groom Urbain continued his riding lessons. The boy was filled with the pure joy of living.

For Henri's eleventh birthday Count Alphonse gave his son a book on falconry. On the flyleaf he had written: "Remember, my son, that life in the great outdoors is the only healthy one; whatever is deprived of its liberty becomes distorted and quickly dies. This small book on falconry will teach you to appreciate the life of the open fields. If someday you should know the bitterness of life, remember that the horse above all, then the dog and the falcon can be your precious companions, helping you to forget a bit."

Henri did his best to follow his father's advice. Though he was still too young to follow the hunt, he never missed an opportunity to go fishing with his father or his uncles. He took long horseback rides. He swam—"like a toad, but well." But with it all—his mother's care, the abundant Toulouse table and the Midi climate, the "cures" at Barèges, Amélie-les-Bains, Lamalou-les-Bains, and Nice —the line marked "Henri" on the wall showed little progress.

His grandmother wrote, "With such a buoyant sprite in our midst, why can't we shake off our fearful dread of his future?"

3

ON MAY 30, 1878, the whole family was in Albi for the weekend. The day had started with the usual mammoth breakfast and continued with the usual family pleasures and distractions, with nothing to indicate that before it was over thirteen-year-old Henri's whole life would be changed.

He was sitting in a low armchair in the drawing room, pencil in hand, reading and making quick sketches in the margins as he went along. He was so absorbed that at first he didn't even hear his father calling to him from the next room. And then, when he did, the incredible happened.

Before the eyes of his mother and grandmother, before they could so much as reach out a hand to steady him—while he was still trying to get out of his chair—he fell to the floor without warning. The boy, who a minute before had been as spirited as the horses he drew, lay in a crumpled heap. He had fractured his left thigh.

It was the kind of accident that happens frequently among old people, but rarely to boys of his age. Moreover, it soon became apparent to even the most optimistic of his doctors that Henri's bones were healing like those of an old person—slowly, uncertainly, and accompanied by weakness, fever, and wasting. Though they had immediately put his leg into a plaster cast and traction, it was many months before the bones started to knit. The warm Midi sun came and went.

From where he lay in bed at the château, often in pain, Henri watched the dawn embroider patches of color among the trees outside his window. Wondering if he would ever again sit in a saddle, he listened to the frantic snorts and neighs of the horses in the courtyard below, as they waited for the Black Prince's whip to signal the start of the hunt. He identified the familiar daily sounds of servants beginning their work: the ring of the blacksmith's hammer, the thump of dough being kneaded on marble-topped kitchen tables, the chatter of the stable-boys scurrying to their chores. He waited for his cousins to come visit him before they ran off for an early-morning gallop in the woods. But most of the time he was alone with his drawing pencil.

It was a great day when he could hobble to the window on crutches to call down to his favorite horse, restlessly pawing the cobblestones while Urbain held the reins. Still more months passed before he could walk, with the help of a cane and a supporting arm, as far as the stables. ("Marie and I are his 'living crutches,'" his mother wrote. "I return home with my arms aching.") Not until the trees were bare and the ground frosted over was he strong enough to stand the trip to Barèges for the mineral baths, and then to Nice for the winter sun.

But Henri de Toulouse-Lautrec wanted no pity. "Don't cry over me," he wrote home. "I'm not really worth it. I'm just clumsy . . . I receive lots of visitors and I am horribly spoiled."

To a friend he wrote matter-of-factly from Barèges: "My dear Charles, you will surely excuse me for not having written sooner when I tell you the reason for the delay. I fell out of a low armchair onto the floor and broke my left thigh. But now, thank God, it is healing and I begin to walk with one crutch and the help of a person. I am sending you the first watercolor I've done since I've been out of bed. It is not beautiful, but I hope you will regard it as a souvenir from me."

He signed his letters "Your Boy-on-Crutches" or "Monsieur Hobble-about."

It was a long and lonely winter, but by the end of it, when Countess Adèle took her son back to the Château du Bosc, Henri could walk again. Not yet perfectly, but better all the time. Only a downpour could prevent him from going daily to the open field near the Bosc where the army was conducting its spring maneuvers, and where he spent hour after hour sketching the artillerymen and their horses.

It was now just a question of time, the doctors said.

A question of time, Countess Adèle told herself, as she prepared to take Henri back to Barèges for the mineral waters. Count Alphonse hoped his son would soon hunt with the rest of them.

And then, as though to underscore fate, the incredible happened again. Fifteen months after his first fall, while out for a walk with his mother at Barèges, Henri slipped and fell into a small gully and broke his other thigh, the right one.

Now it was no longer a question of time until recovery, but of a congenital bone deficiency which might never be cured. This time it was not certain that he would ever walk again.

Henri was not yet fifteen years old, but he had already painted three pictures which would one day hang in world-famous museums: *Races at Chantilly*, showing himself, Princeteau, and Louis Pascal galloping home from the races in a victoria; *Artilleryman Saddling His Horse*, fruit of the spring maneuvers near the Bosc; and *Rider Trotting*.

"At the moment I'm at Lamalou-les-Bains," Henri wrote to his friend Etienne Devismes, "a thermal station whose waters contain iron and arsenic (but not too much, says the doctor), and I soak myself inside and out. It's much sadder than Barèges, to put it mildly, but at least one can't break a leg here (or at any rate, the experiment has never succeeded)."

The two boys carried on a lively correspondence. It was

hard to believe that Henri wrote most of his letters lying in bed, or in between treatments.

The year before, when they first met at Barèges, Devismes had told Henri about *Cocotte*, a story he was writing. It was the touching tale of a cavalry mare transformed into the horse of a simple priest. One day, hearing the far-off sound of a bugle, the old charger galloped off to rejoin her regiment and was condemned to death. Henri had agreed to do the illustrations and now sent off twenty-three sketches to his friend. "I've done my best. . . . They're only rough sketches, maybe a little too gay. . . . If you want more, I'm your man."

If drawing had been a pastime before, it now became a passion. At his mother's insistence he continued studying with his tutors, but every moment stolen from Latin went to art. He tried his hand at portraits, oils, and pastels, becoming more and more self-critical. As his eye sharpened, so did his standards.

From Nice he wrote again to his friend, enclosing some watercolors: "My menu isn't very varied, I've only horses and sailors to choose from; the former succeed better. As for landscapes, I'm incapable of doing them . . . my trees are like spinach. The Mediterranean is a devil to paint, precisely because it is so beautiful."

He never complained when his mother was with him, seeking rather to cheer her up. He went so far as to assure her that he would miss his cast when the doctors removed it.

But sometimes, in the journal he called *Zig-Zag* and in which he sketched and jotted down the things that went on around him, he wrote differently: "I am alone most of the day, I read for hours, my head aches. I draw and I paint as much as I can, until my hand gets tired— and when evening comes I wait to see whether Jeanne d'Armagnac [his cousin] will come to visit me. She comes sometimes and I listen to her talk without daring to look at her. She is so tall and beautiful, and I, I am neither tall nor beautiful."

The doctors tried everything. The day did come when Henri's legs could carry him again, but they were not and would never again be like those of other boys.

He had no illusions about himself. "Look at that figure!" he wrote, having drawn himself in a letter. "Absolutely a stranger to elegance—that fat backside! He isn't handsome, and after having knocked at the door and brushed past the concierge, who cried out in astonishment upon seeing him, he ran upstairs as quickly as those broken legs would carry him."

He went to Paris in July, 1881, where he took and failed his examinations for the Baccalauréat (high-school diploma), whereupon he ordered new visiting cards from the printer:

Henri de Toulouse-Lautrec
Exam flunker

Then he went to the city of Toulouse in November of the same year, just before his seventeenth birthday, where he took the exams again and passed. "Plunged into the whirlwind of the Baccalauréat," he wrote, excusing himself for a delayed reply to his friend Devismes. ". . . I made it this time. I've neglected my friends, painting, everything that deserves attention on this earth, for the dictionaries and manuals. At last the jury at Toulouse pronounced me acceptable, in spite of the nonsense I dished out to them!! I quoted passages from Lucain, who doesn't exist, and the professor, wanting to appear erudite, received me with open arms."

On his last trip to the corridor wall to be measured, Henri's sure eye detected not a quarter of an inch difference between the new line and the old. He measured about five feet tall.

But while his atrophied legs never grew again, the rest of him did. The head and the torso became those of a man—foreshortened on two bandied, frail stumps like the shadow one casts before one at high noon. The nose grew large and bulbous, the lips thickened, the skin became mottled, the beard came in coarse and stubbled, the hands were overlarge.

Only the eyes remained attractive, continuing to sparkle with intelligence and high humor. They were the brilliant and penetrating eyes of an unusually gifted man who saw clearly and accepted what he saw—himself, everybody around him, the human condition. They mirrored his zest for life.

"One must learn to bear with oneself," Henri de Toulouse-Lautrec wrote to his old friend Maurice Joyant at the Lycée. He was only seventeen years old. He was "neither tall nor beautiful." But he knew what he wanted to do.

By the time he was seventeen, Lautrec had grown as tall as he ever would; this photograph was taken several years later.

4

WHEN HENRI FIRST broached the subject of going to Paris to study art, his family was appalled. It was one thing for a Toulouse-Lautrec to sit in the stately drawing room of the Château and fashion horses out of modeling clay, and quite another to consider art a serious substitute for hunting. The only one who heartily supported his plan was his uncle Charles. With his help, and the intervention of a friend in Albi, Henri managed to get himself accepted into the studio of Monsieur Léon Bonnat.

Even Count Alphonse could not object to that. "My son is studying with Bonnat" was something he could toss off nonchalantly at the Jockey Club. Monsieur Bonnat was as high up in "the art establishment" as one could get. He was a member of the Académie Française and a candidate for the Grand Cross of the Legion of Honor. To be painted by Bonnat, one art critic had written, the aspiring subject must first order a "portrait by Bonnat" gown and then prepare herself by "prayer, fasting, and every kind of austerity." A student who entered his studio was taking a vital step on the road to L'Ecole des Beaux-Arts and eventual glory.

Henri returned with his mother to the town house on the Faubourg Saint-Honoré to begin his new life. He was understandably nervous on the morning when the carriage came to take him to the great man's studio for his first lesson. He had never really "learned how" to draw except during those few months with Princeteau some ten years ago. How could he be sure that Uncle Charles was right about his talent? What if his father, who had dreamed of his being a hunter, were again to be disappointed in his son?

Meeting new people for the first time was hard. He still wasn't used to it. He tried to time his arrival so that he would be neither the first nor the last to enter Bonnat's studio. As rapidly as his legs would carry him, he limped to an easel in the corner and hung his short cane by its crow's-beak handle within easy reach. The stool was too high for him. Clutching the seat with both hands from behind, he boosted himself onto it, feet dangling in air, and looked around at his fellow art students as though daring them to laugh. Some of them did, and he laughed with them. It was the best way. Then he examined his palette, his easel, his paints—the first "real" ones he had ever used—and waited eagerly for "the maestro" to appear.

Monsieur Bonnat was a short, pompous, fussy, frock-coated man who wore high heels and had an air of importance. The portraits he painted (and sold for important prices) were in somber, dignified colors and followed all the rules of classical painting. Neither the exuberant palette nor the vigorous drawing of his newest student pleased Monsieur Bonnat. Henri began for the first time in his life to draw and rub out, paint and paint over, design and erase under the critical eyes of a rigid taskmaster.

In his reports to his uncle Charles he alternated between exhilaration and despair: "Prophet, prophet, dear uncle, rival of Mahomet! . . . What studies in view! . . . Here is the plan I think has the best chances: Ecole des Beaux-Arts, Atelier Cabanel, then Atelier de René. . . . I'm babbling. But I hope it pleases you, because you're the one that lit the crayon spark in me."

Then, only a short time later, on May 7, 1882: "You are probably curious to know what kind of encouragement Bonnat gives me. He told me: 'Your painting isn't bad, it even has some style, in any case it isn't bad, but your drawing is simply atrocious.' And I have to take my courage in both hands and begin all over again."

Perpendiculars, proportion, foreshortening, color values, perspective—these were the words that replaced the vocabulary of the hunt. Mornings he spent at Bonnat's studio, afternoons at that of Princeteau or Henri Rachou, a fellow student from the Midi who was also studying with Bonnat. Five times a week he went from the daytime raffishness of schoolboy puns and dirty songs, French fries and cheap beer, to the evening decorum of stiff-backed chairs in his mother's salon. Weekends he went to the races, sometimes with his father, often with Princeteau and Louis Pascal. He was equally at home in both worlds.

After his first few days in Bonnat's studio nobody paid special attention to the little man in the corner in his black-and-white checked trousers, a soft hat pushed down over his forehead, a pince-nez dangling on a string, the short cane—not much longer than a knitting needle—always handy. When "the maestro" was present he was attentive and eager. But when Monsieur Bonnat tapped out of the room on his high heels, Lautrec's natural spirits brimmed up and over.

He would reduce his companions to helpless laughter with an impertinence delivered in spicy dialect. From time to time he would break into loud song and the others would join in, or he would commit a pun so broad that everyone would groan in mock pain. Or he'd invite them all for a glass of wine or beer after class.

More often he would rip up a drawing in self-disgust and begin all over again. How could he learn to frame attention in a drawing when his pencil kept spilling over the edges, destroying space—or rather creating unseen, unlimited space? How could he harness vivid color against a background of somber brown? How could he paint a portrait that would please, if it meant blurring the truth? How could he deny what his eyes saw, what his mind sensed? How could he force his exploring brush into safe channels?

Years later Lautrec would say, "Bonnat's lash was good for me." But when he returned to the Midi for the summer, he was quick to liberate himself from it.

July shone with all its usual sultriness, and he spent most of his time out-of-doors either at the Château du Bosc or at Céleyran. Spontaneously, with freedom and verve, he painted the life he could no longer participate in—the busy, self-contained world he grew up in. He showed the grooms currying a horse under the watchful eyes of Count Alphonse himself; a farmhand resting in the middle of a field, hands self-consciously folded in his lap; the carriage waiting in front of the gate, the young worker sitting on a wall whittling a piece of wood; a tree-lined walk in the woods of Céleyran. His mother posed for him under a tree in the garden, a book in her lap.

His pencil caught the sagging muscles of an old woman slumped on a bench, and the wrinkled face of a faithful servant under his wide-brimmed hat. No portrait could have strayed further from Monsieur Bonnat's injunctions than the one of old Mathias hunched glassy-eyed over a bar table, face flushed and sodden with alcohol. One by one Henri cast off the rules.

When August turned out to be perversely and persistently rainy, and his legs ached from the dampness, Lautrec set up his easel by the fireplace in the drawing room of the Château. While Pierre the groom posed for

All his life, Lautrec kept returning to his mother's warmth,
and to her peaceful garden, far from his hectic life in Paris.

him, the hunters came in to watch—booted, dressed, waiting for the weather to clear. If he would gladly have changed places with them, he never said so. And perhaps by now that "crayon spark" his uncle Charles had ignited in him was stronger than all other desires, even the desire to hunt.

It was just as well that Bonnat decided to close his studio permanently. At the end of the summer Lautrec went back to the Faubourg Saint-Honoré and a new teacher.

Fernand Cormon, or as his affectionate but irreverent students called him, *Père la Rotule* ("Father Swivel-joint"), was a tall, skinny, bony man with an impressive beard and a casual approach to discipline. The atmosphere in his studio was one of uninhibited bohemianism. Though he himself preferred Greek nymphs to French laundresses and Trojan battles to Parisian street scenes, he allowed his students far more freedom than had Bonnat. Lautrec, now eighteen years old and his mother's boy only on weekends, thrived on it.

Shortly after nine every morning he rapped out a loud staccato with his cane en route from studio door to easel. Everybody shouted greetings, in a variety of accents. Everybody was his friend—from Henri Rachou and the others he had known at Bonnat's to the newest arrival. They were a mixed lot, drawn by the lure of the palette and Cormon's reputation from all over France and as far away as Australia and the United States.

René Grenier, a fellow Southerner from Toulouse, was one of Lautrec's special friends. So was François Gauzi, another son of the Midi, a man of high spirits and original mind. And Vincent van Gogh (the brilliant and moody Dutchman), Emile Bernard, Adolphe Albert, and Charles Edouard Lucas.

The acknowledged leader of the students was Louis Anquetin, a giant from Normandy who towered sixteen inches over Lautrec and was his self-appointed protector whenever the horseplay in the studio got too rough. Because Anquetin had an extraordinary gift not only for drawing but also for horsemanship, the bond between them extended beyond the studio.

Cormon's studio was on the rue Constance on Montmartre, that hill rising above the heart of Paris which, though still sparsely populated, was destined for a colorful future. The neighborhood buzzed with activity and the studio was always crowded and usually noisy, except twice a week when the master made his rounds like a doctor in a ward. Moving from one student's easel to another, he delivered rapid-fire criticism in a voice which was overheard by all the others, momentarily silenced and anxiously awaiting their turns. Cormon insisted on "the rules" and hammered away at the basic principles of sound drawing. Nevertheless, whether because he recognized it or because he was baffled by it, he allowed talent free rein—at least within limits.

The Paris art world was in ferment. The Impressionists were daring to question formulas which had been

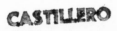

laid down, presumably for all time, generations ago. Edouard Manet, whose nude *Olympia* had aroused the public nearly to fist fights (because the naked lady was real, not a nymph), died in 1883; but Auguste Renoir, Berthe Morisot, Camille Pissarro, Alfred Sisley, and of course Paul Cézanne and Edgar Degas were still very much alive.

"Out of the studio!" the Impressionists cried. "Into the open air!" Artists were to work directly from nature, neither adding to nor leaving out anything which they saw with their own eyes. They painted by the light of the sun: no more trickery, no retouching in the studio. No striving for effects. No more mixing of colors. Black, asphalt, sepia were banned from their palettes. Chiaroscuro, that play of shadow and light so beloved by the old masters, was taboo. The Impressionists sought to capture even the most fleeting of impressions, one single sunburst moment in nature, and make it luminous through the use of broken, diffused color.

These were challenging ideas to the thirty-odd students crowded easel-to-easel in Cormon's studio. They argued about them while they sharpened pencils. Faithfully copying the pose of the model on the table in front of them, they discussed and debated and dissented. But they conscientiously heeded Cormon's instructions. They were here to learn to draw. Anybody who wanted to paint the way the Impressionists did was free to do so—at home.

In theory Lautrec went along with the Impressionists, but he was no more inclined to follow their rules than those of anybody else. Neither in painting nor in conduct, neither in standards nor in way of life, did Toulouse-Lautrec adhere to a pattern set by other people. The changes set in motion by the Impressionists soon began to move in many different directions, and sometime later the "isms" proliferated: Fauvism, Symbolism, Nabism, Cubism. But to Lautrec's work it remained impossible to attach an "ism." Lautrec was Lautrec.

Even Cormon recognized that. He left him more or less alone to do what he wanted.

The oldest model in Cormon's studio was "Father" Cobb, already in his seventies, for whom a whole week during each year was set aside for posing. Père Cobb had made his living by standing or sitting immobile on models' tables all his life long; by now his face looked as though generations of art students had practiced drawing lines on it. He was as twisted and gnarled as an olive tree, as crumpled as wastepaper. Because his creaky old legs could no longer hold him steady, he posed seated on a wooden stool, bent over, arms hanging limply.

Irrepressible, Lautrec couldn't resist his first impulse. He drew a wizened old monkey crouched on his haunches who, for all that he was pure simian, bore an unmistakable resemblance to the unsuspecting Père Cobb. The studio broke down in laughter. Then he tore up the sketch and began to work. Deeper and deeper, behind the etched lines on the face and the swollen veins in the hands, he probed for the life story that had put them there, for the man behind the portrait of the man.

This was what he wanted to paint: people. Not portraits. People. Would he ever succeed?

"I am not about to regenerate French art," he wrote to his uncle Charles in a moment of desperation. "I am struggling with a wretched sheet of paper which has done nothing to me and on which I am doing nothing fine. But I hope it will all go better with more study. I am a miserable worker!"

Nobody was more proud than Countess Adèle on the day when she heard her son's voice, even before the sound of his cane on the parquet floor, shouting good news from the doorway. Cormon had selected him, out of all the students, to work alongside several well-known artists on the illustrations for a first edition of Victor Hugo's complete works. All the arrangements had been made with the editor; he would even be paid for it!

She knew that the money itself was unimportant. But "those first five hundred francs earned by your little grandson," she wrote to her mother, "seem very glorious to me . . . for they mean that he is not the smallest person in terms of accomplishment."

Countess Adèle was not deceived when Henri jokingly referred to himself as "half-pint" and drew ridiculous caricatures of a dwarfish painter to make her laugh. Though they never spoke openly about it, she was acutely aware of her son's suffering.

Every morning she watched him hoist himself into the carriage as quickly as he could and try to disappear behind the horses. She saw him sit up only after the horses broke into a trot and nobody passing by could see his dwarfed legs, the thick lips, the oversized head. Once in the studio he could relax and feel safe; nobody would turn around to stare at him. Face to face with his easel he was as much a man as any of them.

Unfortunately, not all the talk in the studio revolved around art. When the other students began, inevitably, to boast about their amorous conquests of the night before, Lautrec remained silent. He joined the conversation only when claims to virility grew so exaggerated as to bring guffaws from everybody. Then his grasp of Parisian slang for certain kinds of women was as colorful as anybody's. Then he could even try to top the others by announcing that he personally would settle only for a strong woman who had a lover uglier than he was. But it was all sham and cover-up and he knew it.

Shame and the fear of humiliation were even stronger than his need to love and be loved. A patrician, brought up in the adulation of family and servants, he could not beg for acceptance. And what "nice" girl of "good" family, one who would feel at home at the Château du Bosc, would walk down the Champs Elysées with him? Who but his mother would sit opposite him at dinner at Maxim's?

With the instincts of a wounded animal, Lautrec sought the protection of darkness and secrecy. He looked for affection among those as scarred as himself. The first girl he made love to was Marie Charlet, who had never in her sixteen years eaten bread as fresh as that baked daily for the dogs at the Château. She was more at home on dimly lighted streets than in glittering drawing rooms; and so were all the other girls who followed her in Henri's life. None of them knew how to hold a tea-cup properly, but each treated him like any other man. Victims of fate, as he was, they lived and let live in a world where nothing human caused surprise.

It gradually became his world, too. At last Lautrec knew where he belonged. He found it increasingly hard to cross the bridge daily between the Faubourg Saint-Honoré and Montmartre, though he was as loving as ever to his mother. If she suspected what was happening within him, she never spoke of it. She merely waited patiently for him to finish his work for Cormon on the Victor Hugo illustrations, and then they went off to-gether for a delayed summer holiday, this time to Malromé near Bordeaux.

Countess Adèle had bought Malromé some months before. It was a splendid property of 125 acres, whose tall trees screened a magnificent turreted château. Her hope was to provide, at last, "a home of their own" for her family, even though she knew that for Count Alphonse it would serve more as a place to store his considerable possessions than as a home to live in. For Henri it offered a summer of peace and outdoor exercise, a complete change from the winding, climbing, pungent alleys of Montmartre.

The sportsman in him learned to compensate for the

loss of his legs by developing his arms. He swam tire-lessly, rowed, sailed, and fished. He spent hours working out with dumbbells and became an expert marksman with the bow and arrow his father sent him. If he couldn't ride horses he could at least drive them, and he went on long excursions in the carriage through the beautiful countryside. And he painted—continuously and with ardor. He did one more landscape, his last, and painted one more picture of his mother, sitting deep in thought at the breakfast table, her gentle face showing the lines that anxiety and grief had drawn, her hands resting quietly beside the gleaming white porcelain cup and saucer.

When the summer was over he left Malromé for Mont-martre—alone. For the rest of his life, except for the briefest of interludes, he never lived anywhere else.

5

BY THE YEAR 1885 Paris had grown to the top of Montmartre. The dazzling white bulk of Sacré-Cœur, the Church of the Sacred Heart, dominated the Paris skyline for miles around. The city planners were busy staking out the funicular which would take future tourists to the peak. Only Montmartre itself seemed determined to defy progress.

For over fifteen years the Butte ("hill") had been part of Paris. The next fifteen years would see the beginning of the twentieth century. And yet, despite the monument at its top and the "colonizers" at its base, the slopes of Montmartre still belonged to the natives hanging on fiercely to their way of life. Their thatched cottages and wooden huts stood among lilacs and syringa bushes, with stringy patches of hay in the clearings between the scrub. Their vineyards, market gardens and flour mills, chicken coops and rabbit hutches, barricaded the way against cobblestones and asphalt.

Now that he was actually living there, Lautrec could begin to explore beyond the low-lying streets where Cormon had his studio, and his friends Anquetin, Rachou, and the others lived. From the apartment he shared on the rue Fontaine with René Grenier and his wife Lily he explored the whole of Montmartre. Before long the little man with the fine manners and clothes, the short cane, the quick grin, and the easy greeting became as familiar to the denizens as their own village characters. He belonged.

The people even more than the place fascinated him. Art students, writers, and actors lived next door to rag-pickers and farmers. Neither the miller's wife nor the pickpocket asked questions of anyone. Some people were hungry, but nobody starved. Most were badly housed, but none was homeless. There was a give-and-take, a casual acceptance, an easy tolerance among the Mont-martrois that made the Butte a safe haven for everyone.

At night the cobblestoned alleys and dirt paths were dimly lighted if at all. No policeman's whistle could bring reinforcements quickly enough to catch the law-breakers who disappeared among the scrub. But on Sunday proud mothers pushed baby carriages up the hill and old women went to Mass in Sacré-Cœur. The hillsides swarmed with picnicking families and lovers. Tired laundresses came to stretch out under trees.

Montmartre accepted and ignored them all. Down below the Butte, in this same year, 1885, the city fathers had just opened the first public telephone booths. Frenetic Parisians stood in line to put tokens in the magic box, merely for the thrill of relaying the latest gossip or singing the newest song hit to a friend around the block. (A favorite ditty was the one poking fun at Monsieur Poubelle, Prefect of Paris, who was campaigning in favor of municipal garbage collection. Parisians immediately made "poubelle" the new word for "garbage can.") But up on the Butte they paid no attention either to telephones or to garbage. Their friends lived within shouting distance. A bit of dirt never hurt anyone. Theirs was a world apart.

Lautrec came of age on Montmartre, though not without psychological growing pains. Attracted as he was to this colorful new environment, he was at first bewildered.

"I am living here against my standards," he wrote to his grandmother, "and I am not used to this milieu. I am uncomfortable on Montmartre where I feel frustrated by the weight of sentimental choices, but I absolutely must forget it all if I want to succeed in anything."

His mother openly worried. Montmartre was "an ugly quarter." She pleaded to his grandmother, "Pray for him, Mother, and for his life in the studio, which is excellent from the point of view of a *métier* [profession], but a cruel shock for a young fellow."

Nevertheless, by the time his twenty-first birthday arrived Lautrec was at home on Montmartre and in the happy, uninhibited, friendly household on the rue Fontaine. One part of him wrote to his mother asking her to send him four tins of his favorite goose livers from the Midi—underlining *"I'm very serious about this"*—while the other part signed himself "a disillusioned old man." Both parts made the whole. Henri the aristocrat and Toulouse-Lautrec the painter had both settled down on the Butte.

Two of the goose-liver tins were for the Greniers. Like himself, René Grenier had a comfortable income and knew how to eat, drink, and entertain. His wife Lily was a buxom, cheerful redhead with freckles, a dairymaid's complexion, and no complexes. Formerly Degas's model, she was completely attuned to the easygoing life of canvas and palette. The front door of the Greniers' apartment was seldom locked.

Lily shared the passion Lautrec had inherited from his father: She loved to dress up in costume. When Louis Anquetin, Henri Rachou, Emile Bernard, François Gauzi, and the others came visiting—waving a bottle of wine or clutching a freshly baked *baguette* of bread—she would often greet them at the door resplendent in flowing Eastern robes, or got up in baby bonnet and frills. Behind her considerable bulk stood Lautrec, transformed into choirboy, Spanish dancer, infantryman, Japanese warlord. A click of François Gauzi's camera to record them for posterity, a clink of their wineglasses to toast youth, love, beauty, sex, art, life itself—and another evening had begun.

Where the circle was animated, its center was Lautrec.

Lautrec, clowning, in Japanese costume.

Lautrec, dressed as a choirboy, with friends at a fancy-dress ball.

His tongue was as quick as his pencil, as vivid and original. If the word he wanted didn't exist, he invented it. He tossed in slang, a pinch of Midi dialect, the latest expression in English, a pun, a quip, even pantomime, to serve up a verbal platter of wit and penetration. He described a florid-faced dandy in seven words: "a lobster dressed up by a blacksmith." When he called a cousin "part elephant," no one needed photographs. An apartment with low ceilings was fit only for "a fried sole" to live in.

"Technique"— that was his favorite word. "Tek-nik," he pronounced it, coming down hard on both syllables. It meant knowing how to make the best use of one's tools. It meant hard work and practice.

Although Lautrec's carousing often went on late into the night, he was at Cormon's studio by nine the next morning. Afternoons he spent painting at Rachou's studio or in the garden of Père Forest, a photographer friend. The garden was unused most of the week and he had free run of it. There was even a little shed where he could keep his drawing materials and a supply of bottles.

Young though he was, drinking was already more of a necessity than a habit. He drank "only a little—but often": one sip after another. While the model rested. Waiting for the paint to dry. He graduated from beer and wine to vermouth and absinthe, brandy, whiskey. Did he drink to forget? Lautrec drank, he said, because he was thirsty and liked alcohol. It was as simple as that.

As simple as the fact that he painted almost every day of his life until he died, because he loved to paint.

Lautrec recorded without comment what his eyes saw, dispassionately but with understanding. And his eyes saw everything. When he went into a tobacco shop with a friend, his eyes were on a level with the cigar box on the counter. While his companion fussed and fumed over choosing a cigar, Lautrec's pencil transferred the expression on his face to the cigar box. Or Lautrec could be standing in animated conversation on a crowded street in Montmartre, and suddenly spot the slope of a tired shoulder passing by, the roguish profile of a street urchin. Out from his pants pocket came stubby pencil and sketch pad. Sitting in a café, he alternated drinking with sketching.

Pages, margins, menus, matchboxes—each was an invitation to his pencil. Like a musician who practices his scales until they ripple from his fingers, faster and faster, so Lautrec learned how to transmit the human condition from eye to paper with speed and brevity and truth.

He and his friends shared many of the same models, and when they ran out of models or grew tired of them, they often sat for each other. Rachou painted Lautrec. Lautrec painted Rachou. Emile Bernard and Vincent van Gogh made his ears ring with theories while they posed for him. Indeed, the Van Gogh in Lautrec's portrait of this artist seems to be in the middle of a sentence, deep in conversation with the unseen person across the table.

François Gauzi was a frequent and patient model; so were René and Lily Grenier.

Lautrec worked with inexhaustible fervor. "I'm an art student right up to my ears," he wrote to his grandmother. He practiced his brush strokes, inventing his own distinctive motion—now abrupt, now dragging. He learned to capture motion with such accuracy that the hand he painted has barely come to rest in the lap, the mouth seems about to speak.

His first portrait of François Gauzi, while sensitive and deep, is motionless. A later one has such immediacy that Gauzi could have walked through the half-open door this minute, without having had time yet to turn around. Lautrec's portrait of Lily Grenier in flowing Japanese kimono is sultry, ample, barely contained. One wonders what Lily is thinking about.

"Tek-nik."

He would soon be ready to leave Cormon's studio.

Montmartre was fighting a losing battle for its rabbits and vineyards. Already the boulevard at the foot of the hill was alive with dance halls and cafés, where people from all over Paris came to drink, gawk, and be entertained. For Rodolphe Salis, an enterprising character, the time was ripe to launch a new venture. In 1881 he opened le Chat Noir ("The Black Cat"), and by so doing sealed Montmartre's future. As he himself modestly put it, "God created the world, Napoleon instituted the Legion of Honor, I made Montmartre."

Le Chat Noir was a *café-chantant*, a singing-café, which was what made it different. Salis had a brilliant inspiration: he persuaded a group of young avant-garde poets, singers, and musicians to abandon the other side of Paris and come up to perform on Montmartre, in exchange for tips from the customers and beer on the house. Le Chat Noir was an overnight success.

But Lautrec didn't much like it. He considered Salis, who had the reputation of never returning the umbrellas people left behind by mistake, an "operator" and a bit of a phony. Lautrec preferred to take his cronies and his sketch pad next door to l'Elysée Montmartre, where beautiful girls dressed in frothy underwear and low-cut gowns danced the quadrille, or he walked up steep cobblestoned streets to le Moulin de la Galette.

Here, on a Sunday afternoon, whole families came from the neighborhood, dressed in their finest. The older children danced while the younger ones sat with their parents around tables in the garden, sipping soft drinks and eating *galettes*, the round flat cakes which were a specialty of the house. Le Moulin de la Galette oozed decorous gentility.

Then in 1885 Rodolphe Salis and le Chat Noir moved out of Montmartre to more elegant quarters. Aristide Bruant bought the old café, changed its name to le Mirliton ("Doggerel"), and moved in. From then on Lautrec's friends knew where to find him after dark. What le Mirliton had that le Chat Noir didn't was Aristide Bruant.

Bruant was then thirty-five years old and had been poor most of his life. Lautrec was barely twenty-one and had grown up in the elegant Château du Bosc. Between them, however, were the bonds of mutual respect based on talent and honesty, and a rare ability to see and accept.

Bruant meant every word of the sign he put up in le Mirliton: "For people who like to be told off." His gift for song and rhyme was equaled only by his capacity for insolence. "Scoundrel," "Prostitute," "Cutthroat," "Sonofabitch," he would greet his customers when they arrived. "Pigs," he would shout at them when they left. And all Paris loved it. People thronged to his doors for the pleasure of being insulted and of listening to his bawdy songs about underworld characters and girls he called "flowers of the asphalt." He sang in a voice loud enough to tumble the walls of Jericho. Everybody joined in the chorus. "Try to bawl in time," he screamed at them.

They were jammed elbow-to-elbow around tables, beer bottles everywhere, tobacco smoke rising to the ceiling. Suddenly the door would open. "Silence, gentlemen," Bruant would shout, "here comes the great painter Toulouse-Lautrec with one of his friends and a punk I don't know."

With dignity, Lautrec would tap a way with a cane through the crowd to his special table. Off came the top of the beer bottle that was waiting for him. Out came the pencil and sketch pad. Lautrec was into another night of doing what he loved most: drinking and drawing.

Some years later, when Bruant had moved to les Ambassadeurs—the "Ambass," everybody called it—Lautrec would electrify the walls of Paris with his posters of the big man dressed in a ribbed-velvet suit, flowing cape, and high boots, a flamboyant red scarf around his neck, his cheeks clean-shaven in contrast to everyone else's beard. But it was at le Mirliton that he began learning "the art of the streets"—art meant to be seen, and not just by snobs or collectors.

Lautrec illustrated the sheet music for many of the songs Bruant wrote. He was also a frequent contributor to *Le Mirliton,* a journal of wit, art, and satire which Bruant published at irregular intervals. And it was on the walls of Bruant's café that some of Lautrec's paintings were first publicly shown.

Those walls were a far cry from the stately halls in which the art establishment sponsored its annual exhibit called the Salon des Artistes Français. Any young painter "good" enough to have one of his works accepted for the Salon was practically assured of "a little butter on his spinach," as the saying went. From there to a professorship or a well-paid portrait commission was an easy step.

Though Lautrec and his friends scoffed at the Establishment, they went in a group to the opening of the Salon in which Cormon was exhibiting. The huge halls swarmed with elegant visitors. Some of the younger painters, standing on high ladders, were still putting the finishing touches to their canvases. Other painters, whose spinach had been well buttered for years, were explaining

Ambassadeurs: Aristide Bruant is one of Lautrec's many posters of his friend. Color lithograph, 59″ x 39½″, made in 1892.

the fine points of technique to the crowds admiring their works.

Everyone could tell they were painters. Over their wide trousers they all wore velvet smocks buttoned up to the chin. Flowing cravats in bright colors spilled over their lapels. Soft, wide-brimmed, floppy hats topped their long wavy hair. Their women, often former models, were dressed in "creations," with elaborate pearl ornaments in their hairdos and hats.

Lautrec led his noisy band through the crowded halls with as much gusto as he had once galloped his cousins across the third floor of the Château. They were looking for Cormon's painting. They found it without difficulty. *The Conquerors of Salamine*, portraying nude Greek women dancing in front of victorious soldiers and waving palm branches, occupied a place of honor.

Lautrec stood back on his heels and craned his neck to see. "The boss is well-placed," he said, an opinion to which no one could take exception. He predicted that the cavorting women would run off with the grand prize. They did.

Having suggested an appropriate gift for the maestro, Lautrec wrote his mother, "We presented Cormon with a ridiculous silver palm which he received with much emotion." Shortly thereafter Lautrec left Cormon's studio. He had ceased to be a student.

6

NOW THAT HE had left Cormon, Lautrec needed a studio of his own. Neither of his parents was noticeably pleased at the idea. Count Alphonse insisted that if he must have a studio, he should rent one near the Arc de Triomphe, a more "elegant" quarter than Montmartre. Countess Adèle was worried about "what went on" in an artist's studio, though she was somewhat reassured when her son told her he would only work there. For living quarters he would share an apartment with Dr. Henri Bourges, a childhood friend who was now an eminently respectable young intern. The apartment was on the rue Fontaine, practically next door to the Greniers. Countess Adèle hoped that Dr. Bourges and the Greniers would keep an eye on Henri.

As it turned out, her son—for all that he was "a loner" —was surrounded by friends. The studio, on the corner of the rue Tourlaque and the rue Caulaincourt, was in a building almost entirely occupied by people he knew. François Gauzi lived on the top floor under the roof. Zandomeneghi, an ardent Impressionist, was on the first floor. And across the hall from "Zando" lived Suzanne Valadon with her mother and son. Countess Adèle felt better about the whole thing.

She might have been less reassured had she actually seen the studio. Its two outstanding features were dust and incredible disorder. Lautrec had told the cleaning woman not to touch anything. Her duties were strictly limited to lighting the stove and dusting (lightly) the small area between his easel and the model's table.

The studio had one huge room and a small one below, reached by an inside staircase and reserved by Count Alphonse for his acquisitions. Visitors who arrived puffing after four flights of stairs were greeted with solemn courtesy by the bearded dwarf with the monocle and the slouchy felt hat. On a table near the entrance stood a stunning display of bottles and all the accessories of a bar. (In the concocting of cocktails, the newly imported novelty from America, Lautrec was an expert.) Nearby was an antique cabinet whose cluttered inside held everything from lacquered helmets, ballet shoes, and old newspapers to Japanese scrolls, dumbbells, and soda-water siphons. The Persian ceramics were a gift from Count Alphonse. The Oriental carpets, which covered the divan, and the Chinese drapes were the result of hours spent in hole-in-the-wall shops. Two chairs, two footstools, and a café table made of zinc completed the furnishings for the guests.

And then there was the huge easel and a ladder nine feet high, with ladies' headgear and clowns' hats strewn over the rungs. The model's table in the center of the room was littered with drawing materials, books, newspapers, tracing paper. An enormous unframed canvas depicting classical Muses was nailed to the wall like a frieze. Produced in two afternoons by the students in Cormon's studio under Lautrec's direction, it was unmistakably a parody on a painting by Puvis de Chavannes entitled *The Sacred Grove of the Arts and the Muses.* The original had been a sensation in the Salon a few years before.

Lautrec the sportsman kept a rowing machine in the studio. Lautrec the gourmet stocked the wines, truffles, and pâté de foie gras his mother kept sending from the Midi. Lautrec the painter piled canvas on canvas, stacks of them, testimony to unceasing work. It was Lautrec the bookkeeper who began to have problems.

"I intended to write you only a simple postcard," he admitted in a letter to his mother, "but Monsieur Dufour having this morning collected (from the verb 'to collect') the payment for the first of the year, that is, the three months in advance, the result has been a considerable diminution of my finances. I'm not broke, but would be if I paid what I owe."

It was a new and annoying experience. The letters flowed.

"Papa has given me some money, but I don't know whether I'm going to have enough to pay my rent and live on it, too. In which case you will help me, if it pleases Your Ladyship."

And again: "A serious question. If Papa doesn't come across with my rent (which it doesn't look like he will), I am counting on you. I'll telegraph you 'Send Money,' but only in case of emergency, which will mean send the necessary 335 francs, 33 centimes, by telegraph (to 27 rue Caulaincourt)."

It was a good thing that Dr. Bourges shared the apartment—and the emergencies—on the rue Fontaine. They made a peaceful household of two, actually three, counting Léontine the cook.

The doctor posed for the painter and the painter made rounds with the doctor. Lautrec's interest in medicine was acute, perhaps because his own health—despite his seemingly boundless energy—was as precarious as ever. The fat, calm Dr. Bourges cheerfully dispensed pills. He took good care of his friend. He worried over his drinking and took the endless pranks and wisecracks with good humor.

It was much harder for Léontine, much as she loved cooking dinner for the two men and their frequent guests, to put up with some of Lautrec's antics. They were sometimes shocking even for Montmartre—like the time a lady guest sat at the table nude. But just when Léontine felt like leaving, "Monsieur le Comte" would offer a gracious compliment and a generous tip. Too generous—like the "loans" he handed out to friends (the penniless Van Gogh in particular). It was no wonder his books didn't balance.

Those were his happiest years, the busiest, the most active. The canvases kept piling up in his studio. Everything was his subject, everybody was his model—including the young woman on the first floor. From the moment "Zando" introduced her, Suzanne Valadon invaded his life.

Her real name was Marie Clémentine Valade. She was three years younger than Lautrec, with claws well sharpened for survival. At eleven, the age when Henri and his cousins were playing with expensive miniature carriages imported from England, she was already apprenticed to a dressmaking house. By the time Lautrec graduated from high school she had been errand girl, nursemaid, waitress in a cheap restaurant, and circus acrobat. Now she supported her mother and three-year-old son (illegitimate, like herself) by washing other people's dirty linen. She supplemented the puny wages of a laundress by modeling.

One day when she was delivering shirts to the famous Puvis de Chavannes, he noticed her insolent, natural beauty and grace and asked her to pose for him. (Though Lautrec didn't know it when he and his friends produced their parody of *The Sacred Grove*, Marie was one of the Muses.) She went on to pose for Degas, Renoir, Zandomeneghi—and then Lautrec.

The guttersnipe and the count had a great deal in common. Marie was totally without prejudices. She had learned to look squarely at facts and faces, to swallow what life served up, and to keep her own inner self fiercely private. Like Lautrec, she had intelligence and talent.

The drawings Lautrec discovered by accident in her apartment were good. She had been drawing secretly for years, without ever having had a lesson. Over her protests, he took several sketches upstairs to his own studio and pinned them up on the wall. Who had done them? "Guess!" he teased his friends. Marie? Impossible! So sure a hand, such "masculine" vigor of line!

Years later, signed Suzanne Valadon, her paintings would hang in museums the world over. Her son would grow up to be Maurice Utrillo, one of Montmartre's most illustrious painters. Now, still Marie, she led Lautrec a merry dance.

Their stormy relationship lasted two years and went through as many emotions as the colors on their palettes, from passionate love to repugnance and deceit. Sometimes she disappeared for days. Quarrels were violent, reconciliations even more so. When at the end Marie even faked a suicide attempt to get him to marry her, Lautrec walked out of her apartment and never saw her again.

But her portraits remained, one of them among his most famous. In *The Morning After* Marie sits at a table in front of a bottle of red wine and a glass. Propped on her elbows, she holds her head with one hand and stares out into space. The profile is delicate; the loneliness is all but unbearable.

So was his own loneliness when their affair ended. To forget "the terrible Marie," Lautrec painted and drank more than ever. He no sooner finished one work than he began another. The *Portrait of Hélène V.* is of a young neighbor whose tender beauty had attracted his eye; she sits shyly in his studio, pale and somehow ill at ease. In *The First Communion* François Gauzi is the gaunt, resigned father pushing a baby carriage past the shirts in a laundry window, while the conventional little family in its Sunday best trails behind. *The Laundress* expresses all the weight of the basket on the woman's arm as she crosses a weekday Paris street, her frail shoulders sagging, her body bent forward.

The portraits he painted were alive. Art that conveyed movement was the only kind he cared about.

He also felt that art was meant to be seen. The people who went to the Salon to admire pictures of dancing fauns or overdressed dowagers weren't the only inhabitants of Paris. Lautrec began drawing for the others.

In 1886, when he was twenty-two years old, he sold his first drawing to *Le Courrier Français*, a weekly illustrated journal. People liked it and other drawings followed—in *Le Mirliton* and *Paris Illustré* as well as *Le Courrier*. In order to keep the family peace, he signed them "Tréclau." Count Alphonse had forbidden him to "dishonor" the Toulouse-Lautrec name by signing it to the kinds of subjects he painted.

But his friends all knew who "Tréclau" was. They could also identify the mysterious "Tolau-Segroeg" who participated that same year in the Salon des Arts Incohérents ("The Incoherent Arts").

The exhibit was well named. The group of caricaturists, painters, and sculptors who arranged it were legitimate forebears of the surrealists. And Lautrec's sense of the absurd and satirical was as great as theirs.

His entry was entitled *Les Batignolles Three and a Half Years before Jesus Christ, Painted in Oil on Emery Paper*. (The rue des Batignolles was a street in Paris.) The card underneath described the painter as "a Hungarian of Montmartre who has visited Cairo, lives with one of his friends, has talent, and proves it." Three years later the same Tolau-Segroeg, who "lives on the rue Yblas, under the third gas light on the left, pupil of 'Pubis de Cheval,' specialist in family portraits on a pastel-yellow background," sent another entry to the Incoherents. This one was called *Portrait of an Unfortunate Family Stricken with Pockmarks*.

"My work is getting along pretty well," he wrote his mother, "and I'm busy enough to exhibit right and left, which is the only way to get your work seen."

He was not very explicit about where he was exhibiting. One of the places was a restaurant. Van Gogh, who occasionally ate there, persuaded the proprietor to let him organize an exhibit where he and his friends could take their art directly to "the people." Late one evening after the restaurant closed, all of them—Emile Bernard, Louis Anquetin, Van Gogh, Lautrec, and two or three others, including Paul Gauguin—brought their canvases on pushcarts to the avenue de Clichy and spent the rest of the night hanging them. The next day when the customers came for their soup and French fries, they were astonished to find the walls covered with paintings, the like of which they had never seen before.

The "Groupe du Petit Boulevard," as the artists called themselves, waited for reactions. The clientèle was not long in expressing them. In fact, some diners felt so strongly about having avant-garde art added to their menu that the proprietor of the restaurant soon urged Van Gogh to return with his pushcart. The Groupe du Petit Boulevard came to an untimely end.

Nevertheless, Bernard and Anquetin had each succeeded in selling a painting. Hundreds of people saw the exhibit. It was all to the good. The familiars on Montmartre and in the cafés began to refer to the dwarf among them as "the painter Lautrec."

When he was invited to join another exhibit in 1888, this time of the "Groupe des XX" in Brussels, he didn't hesitate. Exultantly he wrote home, "I'm going to exhibit in Belgium in February and two avant-garde Belgian painters who came to see me were charming and lavish with, alas, unmerited praise."

The Groupe des XX included the most "modern," active, and experimental painters in Belgium, among them Octave Maus and James Ensor. Visitors to the exhibit would not find dancing nymphs, nostalgic allegories, or heroic battle scenes hanging on the walls; they would be surprised, even shocked, at the vivid coloring, which had little in common with the conventional palette of the past. The Groupe sought to provoke scandal and succeeded. In announcing the show, one newspaper exploded: "What is Maus going to show us this time: green rabbits, pink blackbirds?"

Lautrec was in provocative company. The exhibit offered him the largest public he had ever had. He packed off eleven paintings to Brussels and was delighted when they won the most praise. Although the critics decried "his orgies of glaring and dirty colors," they did praise the way he projected the very thoughts of his models onto canvas, and "his somewhat rascally verve."

This time he had signed his work with his own name. Whether Count Alphonse liked it or not, his son was beginning to be known.

7

EVEN THE BUMS leaning against walls knew who Lautrec was and tipped their caps when he hobbled by, night after night, on his way to the *café-concert*—the "*caf' conc'*," as the Parisians called it.

There were over twenty such cafés in Paris in 1888, with names like Eldorado, Alcazar, Ambassadeurs, Ba-Ta-Clan, and Divan Japonais. The café-concert had a real stage, with footlights and a curtain. It was a cross between a theater and a music hall, where the customers sat around tables guzzling their beer while the performers on stage danced in a flurry of ruffles or sang to the accompaniment of a tinny piano.

Everything was dim except the stage. The only illumination on faces, hands, gestures, and gyrations was projected upward from the flickering gas footlights, which cast an eerie, greenish glow, transforming what-

The *Divan Japonais* poster advertised one of the new cafés of the period. Color lithograph, 31⅝″ x 23⅞″, 1892.

ever they touched. Strange shadows appeared on walls, distortions in movement and pose. Unsuspected traits were brought out in otherwise ordinary faces. The theatrical quality which the performers acquired deceived everybody in the audience except the little man in the corner.

Nothing deceived Lautrec's eyes. He sat for hours, pencil in hand—a burned-out match if need be—probing through the green haze and beneath the greasepaint. He made hundreds, thousands of sketches: a singer's hands, a dancer's legs, and faces—those on the stage, those at the tables. His eloquent pencil captured the atmosphere and the mood of *la belle époque*. That's what people called it: "the beautiful epoch," in the pleasure capital of the world.

Already a new phrase flew from person to person: *fin de siècle*: "the end of the century." The last decade of the nineteenth century was approaching. It was exciting. It was frightening. It was a time of ferment, when real people seemed to move as jerkily as the ones in the newly invented *cinéma*. On Montmartre all the passions came together and were expressed in a frenzy of pleasure-seeking and sordidness, of invention and soaring wit. Fortunately for everybody, Lautrec was on hand to record it.

He was twenty-five years old when the world came to celebrate Twenty-five Years of Progress at the Paris Exposition of 1889. There had never been anything like it. Day in, day out, the trains roared to a halt at railway stations, bringing tens of thousands of visitors from all over the world. Everybody headed for the Eiffel Tower.

Two years earlier, when Gustave Eiffel began building his tower, half the population of Paris had booed and the other half had cheered. An eminent professor proved mathematically that if Monsieur Eiffel went higher than the 723 feet he planned, his whole steel monstrosity would come crashing down. "A black and gigantic factory chimney," some called it. "An odious column of bolted steel," warned others. For two years the battle had raged and Parisians had fought it out in verse and song in every *caf' conc'* in the city.

But now they sang a different tune. Workers in blue blouses and dandies in flowered vests joined crowned heads of Europe to climb 750 steps to the top. The Prince of Wales came from England and Buffalo Bill from America's Far West. Thomas Edison the inventor and Sarah Bernhardt the actress and eight kings from Africa all made the dizzy ascent. Jules Verne, the man who wrote about the future, climbed up to take a look around. By the time the Exposition of 1889 ended, over three and a half million people had gone to the top of the Eiffel Tower to marvel at the glittering city below. Thanks to the invention of Thomas Edison, the monuments of Paris were ablaze for the occasion. From the summit of the Eiffel Tower a tricolored beacon cast a beam powerful enough to illuminate half the city. People called it an electric fairyland.

The visitors wore down the heels of their shoes walking through the Halls of Progress, marveling at man's ingenuity. Then, each evening after the exposition closed its gates, people headed for Montmartre to sample the nocturnal pleasures of "Gay Paree," the wickedest city in the world. They felt the need for some down-to-earth sin.

Joseph Oller had foreseen that need. On October 5, 1889, in partnership with Charles Zidler, he opened the Moulin Rouge.

Opening night at the Moulin Rouge was by invitation only. Lautrec was there, of course, with Dr. Bourges and the Greniers. His cousin Gabriel Tapié de Céleyran, a medical student, came all the way from the university in Lille. "Everybody" was there, looking around to see who else had been invited. The champagne that launched the Moulin Rouge flowed without stint.

What was it? Café-concert? Music hall? Theater? It was a public dance hall—in principle. But not many of the clients danced. They came to watch the dancers and the people watching the dancers. Little shopkeepers came and fat bourgeois from the provinces, as well as the aristocracy of Paris. Even the Prince of Wales, a fugitive from Victorian English protocol, paid a discreet visit. As for Lautrec, he was on hand every evening from the moment the arms of the huge red windmill on the boulevard de Clichy began turning until far, far into the night when they stopped.

There was a wide gallery inside, a vast bar with tables

In *Gala Evening at the Moulin Rouge: Entry of Cha-U-Kao*, drawing, 38″ x 29″, 1896, Henri de Toulouse-Lautrec included himself and his cousin Gabriel in the background.

to sit at, and a main room for dancing, plus a covered promenade and a garden outside containing a model of an elephant big enough to house an orchestra and belly dancers. There was also a track for the donkey rides that were so popular.

In the Moulin Rouge, Lautrec found his own private paradise. His table was always reserved for him. Everybody knew him. The regulars liked and respected him and left him in peace; if an occasional head turned in his direction, it was that of a tourist. The orchestra blared at top volume. The stomp of feet was deafening. Between the ear and the eye—and the nose—one's senses were assaulted.

The shrewd proprietors of the new dance hall had lured Montmartre's best talent away from competitors. Every evening a roll of the drums and a crescendo of brass announced that the show was beginning. The crowd grew tense. The dancers arrived. Shouting, whistling, clapping, the customers called out their names. There was Nini Patte-en-l'Air ("Leg-in-the-Air"); Grille d'Egout ("Sewer Grating"); Nana la Sauterelle ("Grasshopper"); Rayon d'Or ("Ray of Gold"); La Torpille ("Torpedo"); Georgette la Vadrouille ("Gadabout"). Above all, there was La Goulue.

La Goulue. "Greedy Guts." Her appetite was enormous, but her waist was as small as a hatband. Her golden hair, piled high in a topknot, kept escaping in ringlets as she gyrated. Her upturned nose was sheer insolence, her plump little body a powder keg. Lautrec's eyes dissected her like an anatomist in a laboratory. Now he could forget Suzanne Valadon.

La Goulue's real name was Louise Weber, and she, like Valadon, had once been a laundress by trade. But there was nothing that recalled the washtub when she occupied center stage, a thousand pairs of eyes riveted on her every movement. For the Opening she wore a sky-blue blouse and a black skirt more than five yards wide. The garters that hitched up her black silk stockings left just enough rosy flesh exposed to tantalize the clients when she twirled. There were sixty yards of lace on her filmy white petticoats; when she held a foot in one hand high over her head, the cascade rippled like a waterfall. Impudently turning her back to the audience, she would bend over double to reveal the heart embroidered on the red panties covering her small bottom. The crowd roared.

"Higher, higher, La Goulue," they shouted when she kicked, kicked so deftly that she removed the hats from the men in the front row with her pointed toe. "Faster, faster," they screamed as she pirouetted. Triumphantly signaling the end of the dance, she did the splits with a resounding thump, coming to rest on the floor with her head high, torso firm, legs extended horizontally in a single straight line. No dance was like the French cancan. No dancer was like La Goulue.

Her partner was Valentin le Désossé ("the Boneless"). Straight as a telephone pole, he seemed mounted on springs. Without moving a facial muscle or endangering

La Goulue, by Henri de Toulouse-Lautrec. La Goulue dances with Valentin "the Boneless." Lithograph printed in black and white, 11 15/16″ x 9⅞″, 1894.

the silk top hat on his head, he danced with the speed and grace of a figure skater.

La Goulue the Glutton and Valentin the Boneless—incomparable pair! Thanks to Lautrec, they still dance today. During the next five years he produced some thirty paintings of the Moulin Rouge, the result of countless drawings and sketches. (To get accurately the angle of a dancer's legs doing a split, he made over forty sketches—a "rehearsal" as arduous as the dancer's.) Monsieur Oller bought one of his paintings and hung it behind the bar.

To the long-skirted or top-hatted customers who leaned over the counter sipping drinks, Lautrec's painting *The Dance at the Moulin Rouge* was as fresh and exciting as it is today. In the background stands a group of Lautrec's friends (including François Gauzi) frozen in attention, while la Goulue and Valentin electrify the center of the canvas. The customers come and go in the huge room, a waiter serves a client, the gas lamps glow. An era is recreated.

In 1891 the owners of the Moulin Rouge commissioned Lautrec to do a poster for them, with results that none of them could have foreseen. It was one of those rare and happy occasions when everything converged: the right moment, the right place, the right man.

Lautrec was prepared for it. He had long since mastered the "tek-nik" of lithography, an art medium which encompassed all his gifts: the vision of a painter, the care of a draftsman, the spontaneity of a man who loved to draw. He was a passionate admirer of Japanese prints, unsurpassed for their color, line, and simplicity. Daumier, "father of lithography," was one of his idols. At twenty-two Lautrec had begun practicing in earnest the process of "drawing on stone."

He went at it as persistently as he did everything else. He soon became expert in producing a drawing in reverse, directly onto a slab of limestone, either with a lithographic crayon or with special ink containing soap or grease. To the pencils and crayons in his pockets he added old toothbrushes, which he used to achieve a spatter effect (*crachis*) in the lithograph. He also learned color lithography.

Lautrec was an exacting craftsman. Any print that came out less than perfect he immediately destroyed. Those he was satisfied with he signed. Sometimes he permitted twenty, fifty copies to be made (or as few as fifteen); occasionally one hundred, but no more. By the time Zidler and Oller ordered their poster, Lautrec had mastered his tools.

The Exposition of 1889 gave great impetus to "the museum of the streets"—"the poor man's Louvre," as someone called it. Eager to sell to the visitors, the new industrialists of the era plastered the walls of Paris with posters about their products. Every fence and kiosk sang of wringers, sewing machines, noodles, and lamp oil. With such competition for the passing eye, posters had to vie with one another in excitement. People began

77

to collect them. The aficionados went so far as to steal them off the walls during the middle of the night.

The man who had made posters a part of the Paris street scene was Jules Chéret. The pink, seductive ladies he drew to promote beverages or ice skating made his name a part of speech—"The Chérettes," everybody called them; their tender smiles and grace adorned the city. Chéret's poster of two years before, announcing the opening of the Moulin Rouge, had been hailed as a masterpiece by everyone, including Lautrec. Its gaiety and good humor, its swish and swirl, utterly delighted the Parisians.

Lautrec's poster, on the other hand, was like an explosion. Center stage, but slightly off center: La Goulue, crackling like gunpowder. Her white petticoats are like foam boiling over, her pink blouse and yellow hair like exclamation points. She is framed by the angular gray silhouette of Valentin in the foreground, his left hand larger than life-size for effect. As a backdrop for them both stands the audience—a taut, black human frieze relieved by the witty punctuation of ladies' collars and foolish hats. Simple colors, flat tints, daring conception. A poster so original and energetic, almost brutal in its impact, that it created a sensation in a city hard to impress.

By nightfall of the day it appeared, the Moulin Rouge and the artist who incarnated it were the talk of the kitchens and cafés. The name of Count Alphonse's son was on everybody's lips.

Lautrec, though pleased, was characteristically modest. He wrote home that the poster "has been fun to do. I had a feeling of authority over the whole studio, a new feeling for me." And a few months later: "The newspapers have been very kind to your offspring. . . . I'm sending you a clipping written in honey ground in incense. My poster has been a success on the walls."

The orders for more posters poured in. He did so many of his friend Bruant that the journal *La Vie Parisienne* complained, "Who will deliver us from these effigies of Aristide Bruant? One can't take a step without coming face to face with him." When "a new Lautrec" went up, Paris crackled with color and drama. He made thirty posters in the ten years he had left. Though they were meant merely to publicize singers, dancers, books, bars, or even bicycles, they became works of art, bestowing immortality on subjects whose fame might otherwise have been short-lived.

La Goulue was one of them. Perhaps because she lived up to her nickname, "Greedy Guts," she soon aged and grew stout—even fat; too fat to get into her tights; too fat for Valentin and doing a split at the Moulin Rouge. She disappeared from Montmartre.

Did Lautrec mourn her eclipse? In any case, he had no trouble finding a replacement. Jane Avril had already captured both him and the Moulin Rouge. Jane Avril—as different from La Goulue as he himself was from Valentin. She too lived up to her nickname: La Mélinite, "High Explosive."

8

"ONE IS UGLY, but life's beautiful," Lautrec exulted. Painting and drawing, alcohol and women, friends, sports, the circus, café-concerts, horses, food—everything was beautiful except bad weather, and one could escape from even that. When the Paris winter seemed interminable, he went off with the Greniers to their place in Villiers-sur-Morin, or to Normandy with Anquetin, or to his family in the Midi. (No matter how much the clan disapproved of his career, the Toulouse-Lautrecs were a close and affectionate lot.) If the Paris summer grew oppressive, there was always the sea. Lautrec loved the sea. And he loved to travel, especially when it included swimming, fishing, sailing. But most of all he loved—and needed—people.

Maurice Joyant, that old friend of his from the Lycée, was back in Paris managing an art gallery. Joyant and

Lautrec saw each other every day. The years during which they had lost contact receded in their joy of reunion, though it was far from a happy event that brought Joyant to his new position. The gallery manager he replaced was Théo van Gogh, brother of Vincent.

That Vincent van Gogh was "different," even the students at Cormon's had known. A brilliant painter plagued by poverty and introspection, Vincent had found no more peace in Paris than in his own native Holland; no more success in the Midi, where he had gone at Lautrec's urging, than in Paris. In his tragic and brief life, he sold only one painting, and that not in Paris, but in Brussels, at the Groupe des XX in 1890.

Lautrec, who participated in the same exhibit, went to Brussels for the opening banquet. His pleasure in the critics' praise of his own works was marred when one of the Belgian painters began to attack Van Gogh. Furiously defending his friend, he challenged the man to a duel. What might have been an unpleasant event, and was certainly a ridiculous one—the other man, it turned out when he stood up, was not much taller than Lautrec—was avoided only when cooler heads intervened. Upon his return from Brussels he found Van Gogh in Paris, where he had come to rest after a long sojourn in a mental hospital. On July 6 they had lunch together. Three weeks later, at the age of thirty-seven, Van Gogh took his own life. Shortly thereafter, his brother Théo, inconsolable, was in his turn in an asylum.

Eventually Maurice Joyant would own the Galerie

Goupil. Now, making an inventory as its new manager, he found the dusty canvases which Théo van Gogh had accumulated and which only future art lovers would prize. There were works by Gauguin, Degas, Pissarro, Daumier, Monet, Van Gogh, Toulouse-Lautrec. Few customers in 1890 were interested in hanging such pictures in their living rooms.

Joyant's spirits were often as low as the day's cash receipts, and he might have given up his job but for Lautrec's buoyant support and optimism. In spite of everything, life was beautiful. And every day, no matter how disappointing, must end in another evening.

A new member had joined Lautrec's entourage. Gabriel Tapié de Céleyran, who had left Lille to complete his medical studies in Paris, spent all his spare time with his cousin Henri. It was like a reminder of the old days, when "the chief of the nursery" led his pack on a merry chase through the Château du Bosc. Gabriel followed Lautrec about like a faithful Great Dane lumbering after a Pekingese.

Heads turned when they entered a café. The tall ungainly man with a huge pimply nose drooped limply over his small companion. Gabriel was as grave as Lautrec was ebullient. The old-fashioned frock coat he wore and the gold pince-nez—even the dignified way he smoked a cigarette—seemed to belong to another generation. Though he was the younger by two years, Gabriel at twenty-five looked like a serious old gentleman.

"Doctor," everyone called him—except Lautrec, who made endless puns on his name and outrageous caricatures of his face. Lautrec ruled over him, forbidding him to talk politics or have opinions, ordering him about like a slave. But the affection between them was deep. Gabriel was always ready to pose for the cousin he so adored and admired. One of Lautrec's finest portraits shows the tall, sloping gentleman-doctor leaving the theater, so absorbed in his own thoughts that he can't seem to decide whether to drag his right leg after the left one. It is a portrait done with perception and love.

Gabriel Tapié de Céleyran was studying under the celebrated Dr. Péan, one of the greatest surgeons of his day, and something of an exhibitionist who didn't mind performing before an admiring audience. At Lautrec's insistence, Gabriel got permission to take his cousin with him to the Hôpital Saint-Louis to watch the great Péan at work.

A more queasy man might have swooned at the fountains of blood. Lautrec was enthralled at the sight of the surgical "tek-nik." He stood so close to the surgeon that he might have been Péan's assistant. It wasn't the patient who interested him, but the doctor—this tall, impassive man who tied a large napkin over the dress coat he wore even while operating. Dr. Péan went at his work with supreme mastery of himself and his tools. Lautrec's eyes never left the operation. *The Tracheotomy*, product of some thirty preliminary drawings, is

Doctor Tapié de Céleyran at the Comédie Française is Lautrec's great portrait of his cousin Gabriel. Oil painting, 43″ x 22″, 1894.

as powerful as the scene it records, though it is not for the squeamish.

Despite Gabriel's pleading and Dr. Bourges' watchful eye, despite Joyant's concern and the letters from home, Lautrec preferred women to everything but drinking and drawing. At the Moulin Rouge he could combine all three. La Goulue was gone? Now there was Jane Avril to occupy his thoughts and his pencil.

Jane Avril was something new and explosive for Montmartre. She was as subtle as La Goulue was obvious. La Goulue's message was direct; hers was like a delayed time bomb. At twenty she looked too young and girlish to have led so shabby a life. Her father, an Italian aristocrat, had separated from his less-than-respectable French wife when their unwanted child was still a baby. Her mother, mentally unbalanced in addition to everything else, treated Jane cruelly. She sent her into the streets to beg at an age when Henri de Toulouse-Lautrec was conjugating Latin verbs. Jane ran away from home; she spent time in a mental hospital; she was often hungry. But even when she was dodging in or out of doorways, she was graceful. Jane was born to dance.

She got a job as a cashier at the Exposition of 1889 and spent her wages on dancing lessons. Oller and Zidler, those inveterate talent scouts, spotted her when she became a bareback rider in the circus, and brought her to the Moulin Rouge. Lautrec did the rest. He could no more resist her haunting presence than he could his desire to draw it.

How she danced! She was so thin and supple that she could bend over backward until her shoulders touched the floor. She invented her own dance steps, designed her own choreography, mingled a curious prudery with open provocation in her sinuous side movements. Spinning around feather-light, she would thrust out a slim black-stockinged leg in an almost jerky manner, all the time looking bored and detached. Even her clothes were unique. She always wore a hat, even when she danced. Her pearl-gray or black skirt was tightly belted around her tiny waist and flared out to reveal soft muslin petticoats, now mauve, now orange.

There was something tantalizing about this pale, delicate flower with the turquoise eyes and pallor, so different from the hearty vulgarity of the other dancers. The other women at the Moulin Rouge called her "crazy Jane." And Jane Avril was, indeed, different from them.

In spite of her hard life she was cultivated and intelligent. Lautrec invited her to his studio to pose for him. As she sat there pouring tea, chatting about books, pictures, and beautiful things, he could almost have imagined her in the Château du Bosc. Had he been different, had she been different, perhaps—? But these were questions he never allowed himself to ask. For now, he was content to follow her wherever she went.

Jane Avril soon tired of the blatancy of the Moulin Rouge, the coarseness of the other women. She moved on to the Divan Japonais and the Jardin de Paris. Lautrec went along, making posters.

Jane Avril: Jardin de Paris, by Henri de Toulouse-Lautrec. Poster, color lithograph, 48⅞″ x 35″, 1893.

Jane Avril Leaving the Moulin Rouge. Oil painting,
33⅞″ x 25½″, 1892.

His poster of Jane Avril at the Jardin de Paris is a masterpiece of drama and design. Off to the left, waving a long thin leg in the air almost absentmindedly, stands a delicate Jane. Her red and yellow dress is accented by the white of her petticoats and the black of her gloves and stockings. Both she and the stage are framed within the continuing scroll of a bass viol, held in the hand of a musician in the orchestra pit below. The notes of his music, the strange silhouette of his head, the frets of his bass viol, are like the chord ending the song.

There were many women in Lautrec's life. For few did he have such empathy and devotion as for Jane Avril. There was a sadness about her, underlying the surface electricity. There was a distinction and an elegance that defied her past. She too, for all that she was surrounded by admirers, was a loner. The night when Lautrec followed her out of the Moulin Rouge and watched her walking off, a graceful figure lost in thought, so haunted his memory that he put it unforgettably on canvas. This was the Jane Avril he knew.

He could even talk about art with her. Occasionally she accompanied him to Ancourt's Printing Shop where he did his lithography. Together they would stand by Père Cotelle, the veteran operator of the handpress, whose head was never bare—so far as anyone knew, he slept in the greasy little round cap—and watch for flaws in the finished prints. Lautrec did a study of Jane Avril looking over fresh proof: a serious, intelligent, sensitive face in deep concentration. He also did a black-and-white lithograph of the printshop itself, and both the full-caped Jane and the round-hatted Père Cotelle graced the next cover of *L'Estampe Originale* ("The Original Print").

Orders kept pouring in. Lautrec's contribution to the revival of lithography was immense. For him it was the ideal medium in which to chronicle the here and now, and he used it to illustrate menus, theater programs, covers for sheet music, newspaper stories, books, posters. His production was enormous. No matter how much he had drunk the night before, not a day passed that he didn't draw or paint. And not an evening that he wasn't back at the café-concert.

Paris during *la belle époque* was like a rising cake with all kinds of delicious ingredients baked in it. Everybody, whether he lived in a palace or a tin hut, wanted a slice. Came Saturday night, the chimney sweep washed off the week's grime, slicked down his hair with pomade, and took his girl to the café-concert. They drank beer while the next table's patrons ordered champagne, but the show was the same for everybody.

Between acts, voices were raised in discussion. Ideas were born; the air bubbled with more than champagne. Heady freedoms were within grasp. And if technology was the yeast making the cake rise, artistic and intellectual fervor was the icing on top.

The development of the camera had brought art face

to face with photography. This new competition led artists to extraordinary lengths. The conversation in Maurice Joyant's gallery, where Lautrec dropped in every day, was peppered with opinions about "schools," theories, and techniques. He listened; he had great admiration and respect for his contemporaries. He considered Degas a master. In lithography Daumier and Whistler were his models. But as for himself, he painted what he saw, as he saw it. "Say what you have to say" was one of his favorite expressions.

It was only natural that he and the others often portrayed the same subjects, worked for the same journals, participated in the same exhibits. Such were the times and the talents, however, that no two finished works were alike. *The Dance at the Moulin de la Galette* as seen by Renoir was very different from the one Lautrec drew.

"I would like," he wrote to his grandmother, "to talk to you a little about what I do with my time, but it is so very special, so 'freewheeling,' that if Papa knew he would no longer consider me a member of the family."

The fact was, Count Henri de Toulouse-Lautrec spent a great deal of his time in brothels. During those years when the old century was moving toward the new, *les maisons closes* ("closed houses") were an accepted part of the Paris scene. Most men visited them, choosing the address according to their pockets. The difference with

Lautrec was that he sometimes moved in and became a boarder.

Lautrec knew that a wife and children were impossibilities for him. At least now, he told a friend, "I have found women my own size."

It was perhaps inevitable that this life would lead to syphilis. It was a dread disease in those days, with no known cure. The disease would exact a heavy price, but the man starved for love paid it willingly.

The brothel on the rue d'Amboise offered Lautrec what he had not known since the days of the Château du Bosc: tenderness and affection, acceptance and respect. It was the closest he could get to family life. Within those special walls he was "M'sieur Henri" to everybody, "the girls" and "Madame" alike. His every comfort was seen to. Nobody mocked him, and he in turn treated everybody with courtesy and kindness.

Lautrec presided at the head of the table on the rue d'Amboise, facing Madame. He saw to it that birthdays and anniversaries were celebrated as special occasions, with flowers and gifts. Women made wary by experience readily brought him their problems, sure of a sympathetic ear. "*Le petit gentilhomme*" was as much at home in this world as in those others he inhabited—from Malromé to Montmartre, from the races at Longchamps to the dances at the Moulin Rouge. And in this world, too, he painted.

In quick sketches made on the spot, Lautrec captured the everyday-ness of women eating, sleeping, bathing, dressing; the softness of feminine flesh, the absorption of a young girl combing her hair, her unconscious grace in front of a mirror. Some years later he published an album of ten lithographs which he called simply *Elles*: "The Girls." He made over fifty paintings as well, many of them world-famous today.

On their days off his favorite models came to his studio to pose for him, sometimes with violets clutched in their gloved hands for "M'sieur Henri." Often he would offer them tea. Holding the cup with elegance, pinky upraised, they would chat with the small, serious *seigneur,* at ease even if his friends happened to drop in. He was the most attentive of hosts.

None of the outraged morality of his family and public was expressed in Lautrec's painting. For him it wasn't the subject who determined art and beauty, it was the artist. These women were subjects like any other. A portrait, whether of priestess or of prostitute, was the sum total of a life experience. His pencil or brush merely transmitted the person to paper.

"All my life," he once said, "I've never been anything more than a pencil." A pencil, he might have added, as sensitive as a seismograph, detecting buried rumblings, distant tremors.

No one was more aware of Lautrec's complexity than his "sainted mother." Even as Countess Adèle lovingly fulfilled her son's requests for knitted socks, truffle-stuffed capons, or a hamper of Malaga grapes, she was aware of the life he was leading. "For the honor of the name, it would be better if he chose his models else-where than in Montmartre," Alphonse raged; and she suffered and agreed. But then a letter would arrive from her son reading, "Kiss my godmother and tell her that I sympathize with her, knowing how unpleasant it is to be tied to one's bed without moving." She would remember the endless, useless "cures," the creeping agony—and she was ready to forgive almost anything. And when the opportunity—excuse, really—came at last to set up a permanent apartment in Paris, Countess Adèle didn't hesitate. Now that Dr. Bourges was getting married, Henri could stay with her again.

9

BOURGES GETTING MARRIED! Lautrec was personally affronted. It meant the end of the casual *ménage* on the rue Fontaine, where Léontine's cutlets and the Doctor's pills kept his stomach in order; where a night's carousing could be slept off undisturbed; where disapproval was mild and masculine. Now the new Mrs. Bourges was moving in. He would have to look for another apartment.

Countess Adèle had found a place as near Montmartre as her scruples would permit. For all that, number 9 rue de Douai might have been transplanted intact from the Midi. No Paris street noises reached the windows where her starched tulle curtains hung in dazzling whiteness. Nothing disturbed the sunny, dignified charm of a provincial residence which just happened to find itself in the capital of France, a city of two million people made up, regrettably, of "all kinds."

There was a smell of lavender and soap about the place, an aura of lace and silver and crystal. The parquet floors and furniture were polished to a high gleam, as were the copper pots hanging in the kitchen. Tiny old faithful Annette had come along from Malromé to look after Countess Adèle and the apartment. It was she who often opened the door in the wee hours when Monsieur Henri was having difficulty with his keys.

Henri ate most of his meals with his mother. There were usually four or five guests at dinner and he sat at the head of the table, facing Countess Adèle, in the role familiar to him: head of the house, no matter where the setting. Should he wander by chance into an afternoon tea party, he knew how to charm his mother's circle with his worldly manners and fine speech. When his own friends came over, they were amazed at how richly the Midi ran through his veins.

It was almost, but not quite, a return to the sheltered days on the Faubourg Saint-Honoré. Countess Adèle did her best to ignore Henri's late hours and his long, unexplained absences. In spite of everything, the ties between mother and son were strong. Even after Henri moved into a place of his own, Countess Adèle decided to keep the apartment on the rue de Douai, though she herself spent little time in Paris. It would always be there, a home and a haven, looked after by one or another of the loyal family servants who still remembered "the little jewel" running about in the Château du Bosc.

She herself no longer had such illusions about her son, who described himself as "this horribly abject being, who is your despair." She set about helping him move into his new apartment on the rue Caulaincourt.

It was not surprising that the apartment Lautrec rented was on the ground floor of the house next to his studio, where he knew all the tenants, the janitor, the owner, and the neighborhood shopkeepers. This was the first time in his twenty-seven years that Lautrec would be living alone. "I shall have the ineffable pleasure," he wrote to his grandmother, "of keeping the household accounts and knowing the exact (?) price of butter. It's charming."

He plunged into homemaking with his customary energy, enthusiasm, standards, and demands. He went to Brussels to look around for furniture. He bought English "Liberty" prints—the height of fashion—for curtains and upholstery. His pride and joy was the dressing table with a white marble basin that could be tipped to any angle.

For his mother he prepared urgent lists. "If you could make me a present of 6 small-size tablecloths and some table napkins you would oblige me very much, because I'm going to have to stock up. . . . Some very ordinary table knives would also be a great help. . . .

"I'm going to buy pots and pans, etc., etc., and when

we see each other again you'll let me use some of the money you have for me for extra expenses. . . .

"In sum," he concluded, "I'm getting married without a wife."

Which was perhaps just as well. No wife would have wanted to cope with his daily activities and the guests who thronged his weekly "at home." Their astonishing variety reflected the many levels on which he lived and the passions working within him.

One of his passions, which he shared with his father, was the circus. Count Alphonse had taken Henri to his first performance when he was seven, and he was enthralled by the magic of the ring. Even then he had an expert eye for the horses and their riders. He soon became a connoisseur.

He was only twenty-four when he began his first major composition, a huge painting, *In the Circus Fernando: The Ring-Master*. The canvas was so large that he had to make use of the nine-foot ladder gathering dust in his studio. The space between the rungs of the ladder was almost equal to the length of his legs. Climbing up and down was exhausting. It took him two years to finish the painting, which eventually hung in the foyer of the Moulin Rouge.

The *Circus Fernando* is powerful. One almost hears the thunder of hooves as the horse pounds around the ring, goaded on by the ringmaster's whip. The rider's ballet skirt and the horse's tail fly in the air. One

In the Circus Fernando: The Ringmaster, by Henri de Toulous-Lautrec. Oil painting, 38¾" x 63½", 1888.

seems to be looking down on the circus ring from seats high in the balcony. Only half of the clown's figure and merely an indication of the audience are visible. Attention is riveted on sheer horsepower and skill.

Tek-nik. The tek-nik of jugglers, trapeze artists, equestrians, tightrope walkers, lion tamers, trained dogs; the tek-nik of clowns. Lautrec was their passionate admirer and friend. He liked these nomads, whose customs and way of life singled them out from other men. He respected the zeal with which they worked to perfect their art. It was not clowning but clowns that he appreciated; not the lion but the lion tamer.

The Cirque Fernando changed its name when "Boum-Boum" the clown, born Médrano, bought it. When Lautrec wasn't at the Cirque Médrano, he was at its latest rival, the New Circus. What the Nouveau Cirque offered, in addition to wild animals and antics, made the Parisians storm its doors. Was there any other place in the world where a circus included a pool and water nymphs among its attractions? And miniature naval battles?

But for Lautrec the attraction at the Nouveau Cirque was Footit the clown. Glum, sullen, crusty, irritable, surly Footit—infinitely comic. Footit was as supple as Valentin the Boneless, with a face so mobile that the movement of an eyebrow could bring down the house. Every gesture seemed to be pure improvisation, giving no hint of the hours of practice behind it. When he put on a bareback rider's tutu and imitated a beginner trying to jump onto her horse without looking scared, the audience howled. Then he would take off the tutu (and some imaginary clothing besides) and stand in a bathing suit at the pool, hesitating before the plunge, trying one toe at a time, shuddering at the whole idea. He was never vulgar. He was never a buffoon.

Born the same year as Lautrec, Footit lived in London, where his father owned a circus. He was already a brilliant horseman and trapezist by the time he was twelve. It took many more years of hard work and a superior intelligence to make Footit the Clown. Every fleeting expression on his plaster-white face with the down-cornered mouth had purpose. Lautrec, that student of faces, sought out his secrets relentlessly. The sketches piled up.

Footit had a partner named Chocolat. Chocolat's great talent lay in appearing to have none; his marvelous grace was in looking clumsy. Chocolat seemed embarrassed by his hands. He fidgeted. He was all innocence to Footit's guile. Few in the audience were aware of the skill and balance that accompanied their mawkish pushing-in and fishing-out of each other in the pool; the timing of their sallies; the infinite subtlety of the pantomime.

With Cha-U-Kao it was different. She was arrogance personified. No one knew much about her, and but for Lautrec she would be long forgotten. But when she rode a horse, sparks flew. She was a female clown, a dancer,

and an acrobat besides, but it was her expert horsemanship that first caught Lautrec's eye.

At the Nouveau Cirque they billed her as "Chahut-
Chaos," a theatrical name of her own choosing. When
she moved on to the Moulin Rouge she improved on her
own invention. "Cha-U-Kao" sounded Chinese and
exotic; it thickened the cloak of mystery that clung to
her. Valentin the Boneless was heard to say that she was
his best partner since La Goulue. Even Jane Avril admired her acrobatics. As for Lautrec, he was seized by
one more of those passions which, however temporary,
were consuming while they lasted. He painted and
drew her over and over again.

He shows Cha-U-Kao dressed always in her circus
costume with the wide yellow ruche around her low-cut
neckline. The white wig ending in a point, with yellow
ribbons tied in it, complements the creamy face and
shoulders. The dark-green bloomers are tight at the
knees; the stockings match them. She looks defiantly
sure of herself, whether she's striding into the Moulin
Rouge arm in arm with a friend or riding in triumphantly on a donkey, escorted by performers in uni-
forms.

Lautrec was fascinated with Cha-U-Kao until Loïe
Fuller, the newest star in Paris, claimed his attention.
Then he transferred himself and his sketch pad from
the Noveau Cirque to the Folies-Bergère. Night after
night found him sketching this latest sensation, whose
talent lay in raising clouds of filmy veils by gyrating

Clown, by Henri de Toulouse-Lautrec, shows Cha-U-Kao in a quiet moment. Color lithograph from *Elles*, series of ten lithographs; 20¾″ x 15⅞″, 1896.

from the waist up, while the projector sprayed colored lights over her. When Lautrec was ready to translate his drawings into lithographs, he went to Ancourt's Printing Shop.

Lautrec spent many hours at the printing press experimenting and exploring. One day he wrote to his mother, "I've just invented a new process that can bring me quite a bit of money." The second part of his claim was exaggerated, but the first part was true. Working together with his friend Charles Maurin, a painter and etcher, Lautrec created a new process of shooting paint from a pistol directly onto the lithographic stone. The wonderful spatter effects he achieved surpassed the old toothbrush method.

He also, in this same busy year, helped to found a new periodical. *L'Escarmouche* ("The Skirmish") was lively, but not very robust. It survived just long enough to publish twelve lithographs by Lautrec, which he grouped under the general title of *This I Have Seen*. They were mostly portrayals of stars and scenes from the current theater productions being offered in Paris. To all the other things which made life exciting Lautrec had added the theater.

The Comédie Française, with its musty old boxes and elderly attendants, delighted him. But so did the other theaters, from the traditional to the avant-garde. Lautrec published an album of thirteen black-and-white lithographs of actors and actresses, including the famous Sarah Bernhardt. He illustrated theater programs. "I have even," he announced, "made my debut in a new line, that of stage designer."

When his friend Lugné-Poë, the famous actor and director of the experimental Théâtre de l'Oeuvre, asked him to do the set for *The Toy Cart*, Lautrec readily agreed and painted the backdrop as well. Unhappily the play, adapted from the Hindi, was not very good. But everyone agreed that Lautrec's set was splendid. Its main feature was a large likeness of an elephant, for which the outsized one in the garden of the Moulin Rouge had served as model.

10

"HERE, LITTLE EXCITEMENT except for a traffic jam, such that I crossed the boulevard with an officer of the police pulling the horse of my carriage by the nose . . . holding back a roaring, red-faced crowd that reminded me a little of a riot. Very amusing, too."

If it had not been for the policeman, Lautrec's cab driver might never have made it across the boulevard. What Paris needed were traffic laws. Between the crowds and the cyclists, it was worth one's life to walk on the streets.

The bicycle had come a long way since the first rubber-tired sensation raced down the Champs Elysées. "The little queen of the road," as they called it in the nineties, was on the way to transforming the lives of the Parisians. Its impact was felt on customs, modesty, dress, language—even romance. (The tandem, "the bicycle built for two," was alarmingly popular. And a classified ad in a daily newspaper announced that "a woman cyclist, 45 years old, seeks marriage with a gentleman who owns a bicycle.")

Not everyone was delighted with the bicycle. Cries of alarm were raised when bold "cyclewomen" took to wearing pants when they went touring. Moralists thundered so righteously at this "third sex" that the Prefect of Police forbade women to wear trousers within the city limits. But edicts couldn't stop progress.

The bicycle had become an accepted means of transportation. The rider behind the handlebars didn't have to be rich. Almost anyone could "drive" to work or tour the countryside for fresh air. Only Lautrec, with his legs, couldn't ride a bicycle. Nevertheless, cycling as a sport—and the cycle-racing fraternity—became one of his keenest interests and pleasures.

Tristan Bernard, the manager of the track at the Vélodrome Buffalo, was two years younger than Lautrec. He had begun his career as a lawyer, but soon abandoned the courtroom for the locker room. He supplemented his income as track manager by writing funny stories and editing a cycling paper. Every Sunday he and Lautrec met for lunch and then went to the Vélodrome Buffalo. Through Bernard, Lautrec got to know all the champion cyclists of the day. Along with the rest of the crowd in their bowler hats and knickerbockers (standard sporting gear for men in *la belle époque*), he watched Zimmerman, Jimmy Michael,

Choppy, and the others pedaling furiously in their multicolored jerseys. Their legs went like pistons. They clung to the steep-angled sides of the track, then fanned out in the straightaway. The yelling, flag-waving crowd behind the barriers was part of the spectacle.

As Bernard's friend, Lautrec had free access not only to the track but to the locker rooms. He watched the cyclists getting rubdowns. He listened to the last-minute instructions of their trainers. Then, trotting behind them as they strode out to the track, he found a bit of grass, sat down cross-legged, and reached into his pocket for his pencil.

It was taken for granted that Lautrec should accompany the championship team when it went to race in England. The day they left, Paris's main railroad station was bedlam. Cyclists, managers, trainers, and bicycles could hardly make their way to the boat train through the crowds seeing them off, yelling *"Bon voyage!"* and *"Pour la gloire de la France!"*

In London Lautrec drank and filled pages with drawings. Then he hurried home to do a poster for "Spoke," the French agent for Simpson bicycle chains and Michael bicycles. Lautrec had to do his poster twice before Spoke was satisfied, but the result was more lasting than the Simpson chain.

The artist tried to convert all his friends into cycling enthusiasts, including his long-suffering cousin Gabriel. Lautrec was the only one who couldn't ride, but putting on a yachtsman's cap, he went to work on his studio rowing machine—so strenuously that the neighbors complained of the noise. It sounded, one of them said, like a flour mill grinding wheat. What did he do up there, make his own bread?

Actually, the neighbor wasn't far wrong. Bake his own bread, no—but he did love to cook. The dishes Lautrec invented or perfected were so numerous that Joyant collected them into a cookbook. He could have entitled it *Tek-nik in the Kitchen.*

Steak should be rare. The recipe for "Steak à la Toulouse"? Take three steaks and place them one on top of the other. Broil. Throw out top and bottom steaks, season middle steak, and eat.

Bouillabaisse: The first rule was that no one but a son of the Midi should try making this delectable fish soup. Henri mixed his own subtle alchemy of spices and brooded over the pot like a witch.

Lautrec expressed his culinary opinions with flat authority. A leg of lamb had to cook for seven hours. There could be no substitutes in the kitchen; butter had to be butter. Vegetables should be picked, preferably, within the hour. Wines, only of the best vintage. On a boat trip down the coast of France, he went so far as to have his own supplies brought aboard the steamer —from olive oil to greens, from garlic to burgundy. He spent most of the trip in the ship's galley, emerging only to replenish the supply of fresh seafood. Fortunately, the sea was calm, or the overfed, drunken sailors might have had trouble negotiating the passage.

Calm sea or rough sea, Lautrec loved swimming, sailing, yachting, and fishing. He was expert in all of them. There wasn't a year in his life when he didn't spend some time on or near the sea, whether it was at Arcachon or Taussat (near enough to Malromé so he could pay his mother a quick visit) or on longer trips to England and Spain. "If I don't smell of codfish I'll be lucky," he once wrote to his mother.

He was irrepressible, full of humor. "Our trip was wonderful, on a sea smooth as a pond. Which didn't prevent Fabre, who went with us, from puking his guts out. There's imagination for you!"

He was adventurous, curious. "I've just been deep-sea fishing," he wrote. "It's extraordinary . . . they throw back into the sea by the shovelful 400 francs' worth of unwanted fish a day. They keep only the best."

But, whether on land or sea, Lautrec was always prepared for the stares and derision of people who saw him for the first time. He tried to anticipate their laughter by being the first to laugh at himself, but it wasn't always easy. It was hard to laugh when someone said to him, as he was leaving a café, "You forgot your cane" —and handed him his pencil.

Whenever possible, Lautrec avoided unknown situations. Often he wore clothing that would lend him an air of authority and command respect. (One summer when he went to the seashore he sported a full merchant-marine captain's uniform.)

Lautrec was happiest when he was with friends. He

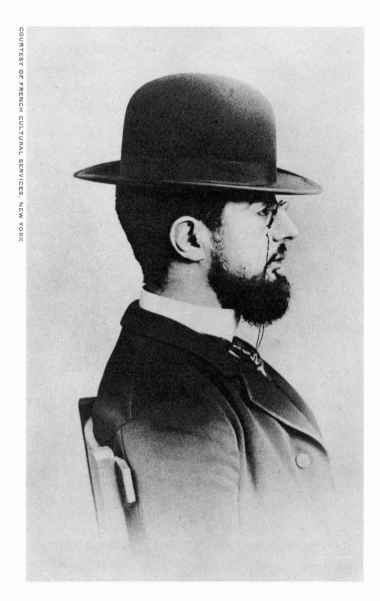

A formal photograph of Lautrec at the age of thirty.

and Anquetin took a trip to Amsterdam together. "We're traveling, Baedeker in hand, among the Dutch masters, which are nothing compared with nature. . . . The amount of beer we're drinking is incalculable, and no less incalculable the kindness of Anquetin, whom I cramp with my small, slow person by keeping him from walking at his own pace, but who makes believe it doesn't bother him."

The gangling Anquetin and the small Lautrec made quite a pair. When the short one leaned his chin on the railing in a museum, pretending to study the picture, it was really to rest. But if the tall one knew it, he didn't say so.

Most of Lautrec's worlds met in Paris, and he reeked far more frequently of alcohol than of codfish. After every brief holiday he would hurry home to the rue Caulaincourt to catch up on what—and who—was happening in his beloved city. Each new discovery produced a new model, and each new model, dozens of works. For instance, there were the two Mays. Both came from across the English Channel. May Milton, another dancer, was a friend of Jane Avril's, who took her under her wing to such an extent that the sought-after Jane would accept invitations only if "Miss" also were invited. Lautrec promptly called the blond May "Miss Also." He became her most assiduous admirer during her short season in Paris. Her choreography was original and her dancing wasn't bad, but her face ever so slightly resembled a bulldog's. Whether for that reason or another, the Parisians soon sent her packing. Neither Jane Avril's protection nor Lautrec's pencil could save "Miss Also" from quick oblivion, though Lautrec's marvelous poster of her assured her ultimate survival.

May Belfort was the other May who would owe her glory to Lautrec. He did a poster for her too, and he timed it so that both Mays could hang side by side on the walls of Paris: one blue, the other red.

May Belfort was a dark-haired, pink-skinned deceiver who called herself "an English lyric artist," despite the fact that she came from Ireland and couldn't sing. Maurice Joyant called her a frog. Her repertoire was limited—in fact, to one song—and her costume ridiculous, but the combination of the two baffled and fascinated the Parisians. She appeared on stage cuddling a small black kitten in her arms. She wore a silly lace-trimmed baby bonnet, tied with big ribbons and knotted on top of her head like donkey's ears, and her girlish curls fell over her shoulders in corkscrews. In a childish lisp she sang:

"I've got a little cat
And I'm very fond of that,
But Daddy wouldn't buy me a bowwow. . . ."

Lautrec made five portraits of this May, who wasn't nearly as harmless as she looked. He took her to dinner, to bars and cafés. He even showed an active interest in her cat, without which her artistic career would have ended sooner than it did. He wrote to a painter friend, "Miss Belfort is asking around for a husband for her cat. Is your Siamese ready for this business?"

Paris accorded May Belfort a long welcome, though it was hard to know why. Maybe the audience liked her mixture of phony innocence and insinuated vice. Or maybe it was simply because she sang in English.

Anything English during those years and in Lautrec's circles was very fashionable. The men in the know wore waistcoats, not *gilets*. A hatter on the boulevard Haussmann printed the address on his cards as Haussmann *Street*. In casual conversation one dropped the fact that one was dressed by Poole, tailor to the Prince of Wales. And nothing was considered more chic than to eat scones in the English Tea Room on the rue de Rivoli.

Lautrec was an anglophile of long standing. Everything about the English attracted him. He larded his speech with English phrases and sang May Belfort's silly cat song long after he had forgotten May Belfort. He took it as a compliment when a friend in London described him as the only Frenchman in all France who could drink whiskey like an Englishman. (He was less pleased when Count Alphonse, responding to a report about his son's drinking habits, said, "Tell him to go to England, he'll be less noticeable there.")

Paris was full of Englishmen, congregated mostly in the Madeleine district. There a sufficiency of bars and restaurants stood ready to fulfill their craving for real

English beer and roast beef when the gastronomic going became heavy on the Champs Elysées. Almost all the coachmen, the jockeys, and the bookmakers were English. In fact, complained *La Vie Parisienne*, "Certain quarters have become so English that even the beggars one finds in them have come over from London."

Among Lautrec's Anglo-Saxon friends, the one who had the most influence on him was James Whistler, who was thirty years his senior. This fine painter, etcher and lithographer was born in America and lived in England, but spent long stretches of time in Paris. To him goes much of the credit for the revival of lithographic printing as an art. Lautrec looked up to Whistler as a master, especially in color lithography. They spent long hours together, poring over prints and discussing technique.

Now, more than ever, neither the days nor the nights were long enough for Lautrec. Without neglecting Montmartre, he was exploring the pleasures of "downtown" Paris. There were so many cafés and bars in the Madeleine area that in fine weather the customers sitting at one sidewalk café were shoulder to shoulder with those at the next one. Lautrec favored them all with his small person. He particularly liked the bars with the high-legged stools which made him appear, when seated, as tall as the next man.

Two places, however, stood out from the rest. When his friends wanted to find him, they went to the rue Royale. Here the Café Weber was for snobs and the literary crowd. Around its tables, theories were expounded, expanded, and exploded in less time than it took a waiter to pop a champagne cork. Writers argued heatedly, journalists with columns to fill made surreptitious notes. Name-droppers gathered conversational tidbits for their next dinner party.

Though discussions were earnest at the Café Weber, no one raised his voice. Ideas floated in rarefied air. And here, too, Lautrec belonged. His drawings for the press and journals, his illustrations for books, made him— more than any other of his fellow artists—a part of the contemporary literary scene. Both in conversation and in liquor he could hold his own. At the Café Weber he drank port, with just the right touch of freshly ground nutmeg in it. To make sure of having this vital ingredient, he carried his own grater and nutmeg.

After a while, however, theories bored him. When the conversation became too earnest, the little man said good-bye to his friends, closed his sketchbook, picked up his cane, and hobbled across the street.

The only serious people in the Irish and American Bar on the other side of the rue Royale were the drinkers.

11

IT DIDN'T MATTER how crowded the Irish and American Bar was—Lautrec had his own table. At the far end of the long narrow room, which was not much wider than a corridor, were a few steps leading up to a tiny square alcove with space enough for one table. This was reserved for the painter and his friends. From here he had a ringside view of what went on.

Not much did go on. The clients of the Irish and American Bar had gathered for one purpose only—to drink—and they went at their self-appointed task without much chitchat or distraction. There was one long row of tables in front of a leather bench backed up against the wall. The long English mahogany bar was polished to a high gloss. Behind the counter a dazzling array of bottles and glasses reflected the light of the chandelier—which was not too strong, out of consideration for the glassy-eyed clientèle.

What Lautrec loved, in addition to Ralph the bartender's imaginative creations, were the customers. The Irish and American Bar was the headquarters for all the English jockeys, trainers, stableboys, and horse traders in Paris. It was the hangout of flunkies whose bosses were eating dinner in the nearby fancy restaurants; it was the waiting room for the coachmen of the aristocracy. (Tom, the Rothschilds' coachman, made it his second home.) British tourists pining for "real," meaning *English*, beer fell upon it like desert-parched nomads on an oasis.

After the Nouveau Cirque ran down its curtain for the evening, Footit the Clown and his partner Chocolat often dropped in for one of Ralph's famous "night cups." Then, if they were in the right mood, the fun began. Sufficiently plied with liquor and egged on by Lautrec and his cronies, the two of them would improvise ecstatic ragtime dances to whatever accompaniment was available. Somebody else would begin a song and before long even Lautrec's cousin Gabriel the doctor joined in the chorus. Maurice Joyant applauded; Tristan Bernard emptied his glass. "Another round for everybody," ordered Lautrec from the reserved table in the alcove. Another round, another dance, another song—another dance. . . .

Lautrec was happy. To the Irish and American Bar he could bring his friends and relax. And drink. And draw.

Some nights Achilles, the owner, almost had to throw

him out in order to close up. Lautrec would make his way with dignity to the door and hail one of the cabs waiting on the street for the night owls. The coachmen all knew him. They kept a paternal eye on him, helped him negotiate the high step into the cab. None of them even needed to ask "Where to?"

The *clop-clop* of horses' hooves was the only sound on the streets of Paris at that hour. The noise bounced off the cobblestones, disturbing an occasional light sleeper behind the tightly shuttered windows of the city. Lautrec dozed drunkenly on the back seat of his cab. The coachman's head bobbed in the front seat to the slow rhythm of the horses. There was no hurry.

Lautrec frequently stopped off at Ancourt's Printing Shop on his way home from the bar. Père Cotelle, an early riser who liked to get to his press soon after dawn, was accustomed to finding him there, asleep—sometimes in the waiting cab, sometimes stretched out on a lithographic stone bigger than he was. Gently the old printer would wake the painter and they'd go to work.

Rolling up the sleeves of his dress shirt, Lautrec fished his lithographic pencil and an old toothbrush from his pocket. No matter how much he had drunk during the night, his head was clear now. He had become so expert a lithographer that he no longer had to transfer his drawing, in reverse, from tracing paper; he drew directly onto the stone. He added a final touch to one drawing, corrected another; waited for Père Cotelle to pull a first proof; then got back into the cab and told the coachman to stop at the first open bar on the way home. He was thirsty.

Now, in addition, Lautrec was busy at the *Revue Blanche,* one of the most scintillating journals in Paris.

The *Revue Blanche* gave space to all kinds of opinions, so long as they were uttered with style. Not all the contributors were celebrities—at least not yet—and not all the subscribers were people of taste; but the average was high. If one wanted to know what was going on in the world of theater, sports, literature, and the arts, one read the *Revue Blanche* and then quoted from it at the Café Weber.

Three brothers with the happy combination of money and a passion for the arts were largely responsible for the *Revue Blanche.* Louis-Alfred Natanson helped found it. Alexandre Natanson was its editor in chief. And Thadée Natanson, a member of the board, was in charge of art news. But the journal had, in addition, a glittering roster of staff and contributors. Its pages were filled by writers like Marcel Proust, Emile Zola, André Gide, Jules Renard; by poets like Stéphane Mallarmé and composers like Claude Debussy. Lautrec now widened his circle of friends and interests.

Along with everything else, the journal was a painter's haven. Art was the special province of Thadée Natanson. He reproduced in the *Revue Blanche* some of the finest talents of the day.

Lautrec's daily sorties from the Butte now included regular stops at the rue Laffitte, where the editorial offices of the *Revue Blanche* were located. His arrival, as chronicled by Thadée Natanson, brought people from their desks to the windows.

"To get to the editor's office, he had to limp across a large courtyard overlooked by four tall buildings. He was never alone . . . but when we looked out to watch his progress we paid no attention to his companion, walking slowly to keep pace with him, but only to the well-loved appearance of Lautrec himself—the little toddling figure, the end of his muffler floating in the breeze, the bowler hat which he sometimes waved to us—Lautrec, dragging his feet painfully across the cobblestones and stopping every now and then to shout something or more probably just to rest; then starting again as if he had never needed to get his breath, leaning on the little stick which seemed as much a hindrance as a help to him.

"As soon as he came into the office, he made straight for a green leather sofa near the door, which one would have thought too high for him to clamber onto but where he remained perched, his legs dangling. Those who had never seen him before, or not at close quarters, were startled by his thick, rubicund lips and the lively spate of words that issued from them. . . . But, while shouting and gesticulating from where he sat, he managed to listen to what was said, and one felt he was taking in everything with both ears as well as with his eyes."

The *Revue Blanche* took its place among Lautrec's worlds, where he felt as comfortable as in all the others.

The people who worked there were his friends. One by one they were transferred to canvas. Lautrec painted them all—portraits in depth of the men who helped to shape the literary tastes of *la belle époque*. He liked them and they in turn shared Thadée Natanson's feelings about him: a man who "knew how to make himself loved, a creature of childlike weakness and amiability to whom one had not the heart to refuse anything. He was both imperious and tender, imposing his opinions, feelings, and wishes on all of us by dint of grace and obstinacy: in short, a beloved little tyrant."

Lautrec contributed numerous lithographs and other illustrations to the *Revue Blanche*. When, in addition, Thadée Natanson asked him for a poster to replace the one Pierre Bonnard had done two years before, he was challenged and delighted. To follow Bonnard was stiff competition. On the other hand, he had been waiting for this chance. He already knew who his model would be.

Parisians had felt the impact of his Moulin Rouge poster; they reeled under this one. The unforgettable redhead striding toward the viewer seems about to step off the wall. She wears a red-dotted blue dress, a hat with formidable ostrich plumes, and a gray fur cape. She looks as though at any moment she will swing the gray muff on her arm right at the spectators. Seeing her, seeing the *Revue Blanche* lettering, no Parisian would be likely to forget either the journal or the lady.

The lady was Misia Natanson. She was Thadée's wife

and as much a part of the Paris scene as the Eiffel Tower or the Folies-Bergère. She had been born Misia Godebska: granddaughter of a Russian prince, half sister of a Polish sculptor, relative of a well-known Belgian musician; a cosmopolitan mix of titles and talents. At fifteen she had married Thadée Natanson.

Misia was beautiful and cultivated, a fine pianist, an avid reader, an accomplished hostess, a patron of the arts. She was also thoroughly spoiled. Her court of admirers danced to her every whim. An invitation to her home was like a command performance.

The Natansons kept open house for everybody who was anybody in Paris. It was an everyday occurrence in their living room to hear Mallarmé read his latest verses, Léon Blum expound on the Socialist movement, Debussy play his newest nocturne. And all the while, Lautrec sat cross-legged in mute adoration of Misia. Lautrec's passions were never a secret, and Thadée didn't mind. He knew that Lautrec would soon be absorbed in his next one.

12

SHE STOOD ON STAGE not moving a muscle. She was elegant, austere, thin, and waxy pale except for the wide red slash of her mouth. Her face was expressionless. But let her just oscillate those long, spidery, black-gloved arms, and the audience collapsed with laughter. One word from her, one sly movement, one innuendo—what *was* there about her? Yvette! The mention of her name could fill a theater. Yvette! They loved her in Paris, they adored her in London, she was the very embodiment of *la belle époque*.

Of all the long cast of female characters in Lautrec's life, Yvette Guilbert was perhaps the heroine. Certainly a leading lady. What La Goulue was to the dance, Yvette Guilbert was to song—and to more than song: to mood and manners, to a way of life, to the tempo and spirit of the times.

At fifteen, Yvette Guilbert had been a mannequin in a Paris dress house. From there she graduated to sales-girl in a department store. Zidler, that same Zidler, with his infallible nose for talent, discovered her and brought her (after a tour of the provinces to learn the trade) to the Moulin Rouge.

But she was not very successful. The Moulin Rouge was too big and noisy for her subtle talents, too raucous and explicit. It was not until she moved over to the Divan Japonais that Yvette Guilbert became a star.

Yvette Guilbert, with her keen intelligence, started early to create an image that would be unique. Because other women painted their lips in a Cupid's bow, she accentuated her naturally large mouth in bright scarlet. Because almond-shaped eyes were the vogue, she made hers look round. A large bosom was every woman's wish. Hers was small. Since everybody wore white gloves up to the elbow, hers, naturally, were black and reached almost to her armpits.

No hat flattened the red-gold curls which she swept upward from her low forehead and then caught de-murely behind in a bun. Her nose ended in a funny lump. Her waist was tiny. Her neck was unnaturally long, and she lengthened it still more when she sang. She dressed with simple elegance—and cunning design. The dress cut low in front was even lower in back. At her waist, a rose.

It wasn't only how Yvette sang, but what. She chose —no, she ordered to measure—her repertoire from the best songwriters of the day. Sometimes they were songs of street urchins and laundresses, sometimes of aged drunken crones and lascivious old men. Or prostitutes. Or young girls in love. She delivered them all without twitching a facial muscle. Other café-concert artists gesticulated and gestured with frenzy. She barely moved. But not a word was lost on the audience, not a single wicked possibility overlooked.

Lautrec had been following her career since the day she began at the Moulin Rouge. He didn't actually meet her, however, until he was thirty and a known painter, and she was twenty-six, a starring singer. He asked Maurice Donnay, a songwriter, whom he knew from the *Revue Blanche* and who composed some of Yvette's most famous songs, to introduce them.

Lautrec was very nervous on the way to her apartment. With his friends he was completely at ease; they no longer even noticed what he looked like. But never, as long as he lived, could he meet new people without anticipating their shock. Even when they knew what to expect. Surely Donnay had warned her?

It was a very proper, very friendly meeting. Only years later, in her memoirs, did Yvette Guilbert describe the little man who accompanied Maurice Donnay to tea:

"I saw a huge dark head, a florid, black-bearded face with a greasy, oily skin, a nose big enough to supply two faces, and what a mouth! A mouth that gashed the face from cheek to cheek, a terrible obscene slit edged by lips that were hugely thick and moist, pinkish mauve in color, flattened and flaccid.

"At last I looked straight into Lautrec's eyes. What

beautiful eyes they were—large, deep, full of warmth, astonishingly brilliant, luminous! I kept on gazing at them, and suddenly, noticing this, Lautrec took off his pince-nez. Aware of his one magnificent feature, he was offering it to me with unaffected generosity."

Lautrec's first artistic tribute to Yvette was not well received. Yvette was as vain as the next woman, and rejected his design for a poster with an indignant note: "You little monster—you have turned me into a horror." But had he really? As usual, concentrated hours of observation and sketching had preceded his design. What emerged was the Yvette she herself had created.

Besides spending countless evenings watching her perform, noting her every movement, Lautrec got permission from the singer to work in her apartment. He studied her wonderfully mobile face, marveling that she could control it so well on stage. He sketched her over and over again, extracting the very essence of her art. He even gave her black gloves a life of their own.

Lautrec's drawings of Yvette on the covers of her songs' sheet music graced every piano in Paris. Everybody saw and hailed his lithograph of her in the journal *Le Rire*. Had he made her neck monstrously long? The chin jutted, the mouth was exaggerated? Yvette no longer minded. She was too shrewd a performer to choose flattery over publicity. When Lautrec proposed doing an album of lithographs devoted entirely to her, she readily agreed.

Yvette Guilbert, by Henri de Toulouse-Lautrec. Lithograph
printed in black, 11½″ x 9⁹⁄₁₆″, c. 1895.

The album of sixteen lithographs was a huge success. The Yvette Guilbert who takes a bow, who backs off into the wings, who flings out her arms at the audience, is not "pretty." She is almost not human. She is an evocation of the theater. Lautrec has drawn not one superfluous line, but it's all there—from the prompter's box to the last row in the balcony, from words and music to tears of laughter. Yvette's gloves alone, on the cover of the album, are enough to recall the songs of the nineties and the woman who sang them.

Four years after the first album was printed in Paris, Lautrec did eight more lithographs of her to be published in London. Among his very best, they put the seal of immortality on Yvette.

Curiously enough, Yvette really *was* a conventional, respectable, almost pious person. The kind of life Lautrec was leading bothered her almost as much as it did Countess Adèle. She constantly urged him to change his habits, in particular his drinking habits.

There was no doubt that Lautrec consumed too much alcohol; even his good friend Thadée Natanson said that the ends of his moustache rarely had time to dry out. "It is useless to deny that," Lautrec agreed. That was one of his favorite expressions. It was also useless to deny that life was short and beautiful and there were better things to do at night than sleep.

And yet Lautrec's artistic production was astounding. No one seeing him glassy-eyed from too much absinthe could have imagined the canvases piled up in his studio. He turned out some fifty paintings a year—an average of four a month, one a week—and almost as many lithographs, in addition to everything else: drawings, posters, sketches, programs, stage designs. He worked quickly, but painstakingly. (Maurice Joyant posed seventy-five times for his portrait.) He worked constantly and without letup, in practically every medium from oils to etching, including brief ventures into sculpture, stained glass, and ceramics.

But Lautrec saw no virtue whatsoever in an ivory-tower existence. Even as a young beginning artist Lautrec had felt that paintings should be seen, not stacked. Whenever and wherever possible, he participated in exhibits in Paris, Toulouse, Brussels, or London. He frequently helped Maurice Joyant and others to organize showings. The object was not only to show, but to sell.

"Foreigners are definitely very nice to painters," he wrote to his grandmother. "I have just sold two paintings to King Milan of Serbia. In the future I shall have to put on my calling cards: 'Painter to the Court at Sofia.' Which would be quite absurd, since the poor chap is already losing political power."

To a publisher in Brussels, to whom he had sent a print: "For you 30 francs, for the public 50 francs. This vulgar detail is simply to make sure you don't let it go for less."

To his mother: "I've seen my dealers. I am to get 200

francs for one study, which means it was sold for 300 francs, a little boost in the scale."

His portrait of Paul Sescau, a photographer friend, brought 400 francs. He sold a print to an avant-garde German magazine called *Pan*. His lithographs and drawings appeared in all the journals and magazines of his day and he never missed the opportunity to do a poster. ("Posters are the only thing," he once told his cousin Gabriel. What a challenge to an artist, to strive for maximum impact with the utmost economy of means!)

Nevertheless, though Lautrec was delighted when he sold something, he was generous with his drawing. Countless were the menus, invitations, and song sheets he designed for friends, the paintings he simply gave away to the people he liked. Lautrec was prodigal with his time and his talent—and his health.

Those good doctor friends of his, Dr. Bourges and Gabriel Tapié de Céleyran, worried. So did all his other friends. Every once in a while one of them would suggest a holiday and, to make sure he took it, go with him. Dr. Bourges and his wife accompanied him to Normandy to visit Anquetin. Aristide Bruant, who by now had made enough money on the café-concert circuit to retire, invited Lautrec to his place at the seashore. Henri was a frequent visitor at the Natansons' summer place. Maurice Joyant took him sailing and fishing on his boat.

The trouble was, Lautrec hated to be away from Paris. Other painters sought their inspiration in seashore and landscape, but for him the picturesque was outside his window, on the street, or at the next table. The most exciting people in the world lived in turn-of-the-century Paris.

13

EVEN THE STREET NOISES of Paris were changing. The
tinny tinkle of the bicycle's bell was losing out to the
chug-chug of the gasoline-driven motor. The automobile
had arrived.

In 1891, by driving from the avenue d'Ivry to the
quai du Point-du-Jour and back, Messieurs Panhard and
Levassor established a world record for distance: five
miles. The skeptics, who had predicted that the infernal
thing would explode, began to be convinced. The timid,
who shied clear of its noise and speed, learned to get out
of the way—though not always fast enough, as an item
in the daily newspaper confirmed: "Marcel Prévost fell,
at St. Germain, under an auto going at more than two
miles an hour. The young man had his ribs fractured."

The kind of traffic jam Lautrec had written home
about was almost a daily occurrence now. There were no

rules. People, pushcarts, bicycles, horses, vendors, hawkers, hacks, and omnibuses all contested the right-of-way and nobody kept either to right or to left: the middle of the road was a perilous path.

As for everything else in those days, there was a prescribed costume for motorists: a peaked cap, pulled low over the forehead; huge goggles to protect the eyes from the dirt raised by such speed; and a shaggy goat-skin coat with voluminous collar to ward off wind. Unfortunately, nothing had yet been devised to keep the engine's smoke from blackening the face. Gabriel would emerge from his vehicle, at the end of a dizzy spin through the park, looking more like a chimney sweep than a herald of progress.

Lautrec, man of his times, conceded that "it was useless to deny" the conquest of the automobile. He who had drawn so many horses in his lifetime now made a lithograph of his cousin at the steering wheel. But for the prominent nose emerging from the goatskin collar, one would hardly recognize Gabriel. His face is black with smoke. His hands clutch the wheel and gearshift with intense concentration. It is man over machine, with the outcome unclear—and as though to emphasize the doubt, Lautrec shows a young girl peacefully walking her dog in the other direction, paying no attention to Gabriel and the future.

Perhaps Lautrec shared the girl's feelings. He braced himself for an occasional giddy ride in Gabriel's car and he enjoyed driving into the country with Thadée and

Cousin Gabriel is *The Automobile Driver*. Lithograph
printed in black, 14¹¹⁄₁₆″ x 10½″, 1896.

Misia, but he preferred animals to automobiles. He still went as often as he could to the Botanical Gardens and the zoo, where he and his father used to spend their Sundays. Deep down, he was still watching from the window of the Château du Bosc for his grandfather to signal the start of the hunt.

Lautrec was a familiar figure at the racetrack and knew all the jockeys and trainers in town. Even more than the cycling fraternity, these men who rode, raced, trained, and curried horses appealed to his deepest feelings and memories. When someone once asked him what he would have been if he weren't an artist, he didn't have to grope for an answer: "A horseman."

Only a man who knew horses could have made the splendid color lithograph of *The Jockey*. The picture generates such power and excitement that one feels like a spectator in the grandstand, jumping up and down and shouting to one's favorite to pull ahead. The horse in the foreground gallops so fast that his legs hardly touch the ground. His back glistens with sweat. The jockey is clear out of the saddle, leaning tensely forward, holding the reins taut, urging his horse on to the finish line.

Whenever Lautrec met his father during the racing season—at the track, at the Restaurant Lucas, or at one of the other fine eating places they both liked—they talked about horses. Evenings at the Irish and American Bar, Lautrec talked shop with the jockeys. These slim, slight fellows were among the few people he didn't

The Jockey. Lithograph printed in black, 20⁷⁄₁₆″ x 14³⁄₈″, 1899.

have to crane his neck to see. Most of them weren't much taller than he was. They had a smell about them which he recognized from infancy. Their slightly bowed legs, their way of walking—a bit like sailors on land—were as familiar to him as the legs he had learned to live with. He could have drawn them with his eyes closed.

The regulars at the bar usually waited for Lautrec to show up before they began their postmortems on the day's race. They valued his opinion. If he didn't come, it meant that he and his pencil were enslaved by a new passion. The year before it had been Yvette Guilbert. This year it was Marcelle Lender.

If La Goulue was the incarnation of the dance and Yvette Guilbert of song, then Marcelle Lender embodied Lautrec's passion for the theater. She was the magic that scenic artifice and artful lighting could create. For her he waited every evening during that breathless moment when the house lights darken and the curtain slowly begins to rise.

She was a redhead, like so many of Lautrec's favorite models—not so intelligent as Yvette Guilbert, not so spiritual as Jane Avril, nothing, certainly, like La Goulue. What all four had in common was tek-nik. Marcelle Lender held her audience the way a light holds an insect. Her grace, her clothes, her personality, her acting, were the talk of Paris. If the comic opera *Chilpéric* played to packed houses, it was due to her performance and not to the merits of what she performed.

Twenty times in a row Lautrec sat in the same seat to watch not the play but the player. Each time he waited tensely for that magic moment when Marcelle Lender danced the Bolero.

By diligent research, he had discovered that after every performance the object of his attentions went to have a late supper at the Café Viel near the Madeleine. He went too, and arranged to have a table where he could sit facing her. He ate his ham and most of the contents of a jar of pickles without once taking his eyes off her face. Even for an actress accustomed to the stares of an audience, his unbroken scrutiny was embarrassing. Only when he had tossed off an entire bottle of burgundy did he ask to be introduced to her. The conversation was brief and abrupt. No compliments, no small talk. Lautrec was saving his comments for his pencil.

The sketches piled up: *Lender in Street Clothes*, *Lender Seated*, *Lender as Seen from the Back*, *Lender in Profile*; Lender bowing, smiling, sneezing, talking, eating. . . .

Finally, one night after the curtain fell, Lender received a huge bouquet of white roses and a note from the painter asking for an appointment. She invited him to lunch at her apartment; curiosity, after all, is human. But if she hoped to discover the reason for Lautrec's pursuit, the conversation around her table offered no clues. The strange little man sat there in total silence, his eyes making her conscious of her own heartbeat. He was like a hunter stalking his prey. She saw him once more, in her dressing room at the theater, and then never again. Lautrec no longer needed to gaze across the footlights at Marcelle Lender; he had transferred her to his canvas.

What resulted was a masterpiece. *Marcelle Lender Dancing the Bolero in* Chilpéric is one of the finest paintings Lautrec ever made. It is also one of the largest; he had to turn his studio upside down to make room for the canvas. The chalky-white arches in the background set the stage. The blue-clad pages and the stiff courtiers—even the fat toreador-tenor in his cummerbund and white stockings—are mere props. What counts is the lady in front. Her costume is startlingly beautiful. She has just come to rest after a fiery whirl, with one leg gracefully pointed toe down and the other bent in a deep bow. Her petticoats refuse to subside; they seem still to be foaming from her spin. Lautrec painted both petticoats and headdress in a glorious pink that makes the figure of Marcelle Lender as exotic as an orchid.

After finishing the painting, Lautrec turned to lithographs: Marcelle Lender in all the moods and manifestations his pencil had recorded. One of them, *Lender in Profile*, he executed in eight colors, a considerable technical feat for those days.

Lautrec went from model to model, "saying what he had to say." He painted the famous actors and actresses

Marcelle Lender Dancing the Bolero in "Chilpéric," by Henri
de Toulouse-Lautrec. Oil painting, 65″ x 59″, 1895.

of his day, as well as the people who went to see them act, and his comments were always pungent and brief, often witty. He drew Tom, the Rothschilds' coachman, sitting uncomfortably in *A Box at the Theater* next to two women of doubtful virtue. His friend Charles Conder, the English painter, he placed next to an extravagantly hatted lady with opera glasses in *Theater Box with Gilded Mask*. He showed the *Chic People* in a fancy restaurant and the thin, greenish-complexioned *Cashier* in a popular-priced bistro.

Never an unnecessary line. The empty spaces in Lautrec's drawings were as important as the central figure. He often brushed in only one person, or one specific scene, merely indicating the setting with a quick suggestion: the railing which separated audience from orchestra pit; a table, part of the wall, a hint of outdoors. The secret of his brevity was focus. Eliminate the extraneous, say what you have to say.

"Really," he once said to Gabriel, "people are a great bore. They insist on my finishing things. All I want to do is paint what I see. Anyone can finish off a painting."

Besides, there was no time for the unimportant. Lautrec was short of time these days. Between the working and the drinking, and the many worlds he walked among, he was the busiest man on the Butte.

14

"WHATEVER HAPPENED TO La Goulue?" someone occasionally asked, usually over a beer with other old-timers.
Only six years after the opening of the Moulin Rouge,
La Goulue was all but forgotten. The dazzling creature
whose wiggle the Prince of Wales had crossed the
Channel to see had all but vanished from the Butte.
Her gold francs were squandered, her figure was gone,
even her memories were becoming blurred by alcohol.
At twenty-five, "the toast of Montmartre" was a penniless, fat old woman. To support herself she opened a
booth at a street carnival that moved from neighborhood
to neighborhood for a few weeks at a time. Because of
her girth, she had become a belly dancer.

The letter she wrote to Lautrec was pathetic:

Dear friend,
I am coming to see you on Monday the 8th, at
2 in the afternoon. I have a booth at the Trône,

on the right as you come in, it's a very good place and I would be most grateful if you could find the time to paint me something—tell me where to get the canvases, I'll bring them the same day.

La Goulue

She knew her friend. Lautrec responded generously with two large panels, each three yards square. The first represented her past: *La Goulue and Valentin Dancing at the Moulin Rouge.* The second depicted her present: *La Goulue in Her Booth as a Dancing Girl.* Looking at them today, in the Jeu de Paume museum in Paris where they hang, one suspects that Lautrec himself was filled with nostalgia as he painted them. Even for him they must have recalled those gilded nights at the Moulin Rouge, when all Paris came to see the Glutton and the Boneless One dance.

The panels were, in the words of the journal *Fin de Siècle,* a *succès fou,* "a wild success." They brought customers to La Goulue's booth at the fair who were drawn more by the paintings than the performance.

Lautrec went to the carnival on the day it opened and brought his entourage with him. Gallantly he tipped his hat and raised his miniature cane in salute to La Goulue. It was like saying good-bye to an era. He never saw her again. Valentin was there, too—as lanky as ever, as boneless, but decidedly depressed. He greeted the painter sadly.

These days Valentin still haunted the Moulin Rouge, but only as an onlooker. He had retired and become a landlord on the money Zidler had paid him. During the day he collected rent for the rooms near the Ecole Militaire that he let out to army officers. Evenings he came back to the scene of his triumphs, muttering darkly that there was no longer anyone who could dance like La Goulue. Jane Avril called him "a worn-out Don Quixote."

Most of the other dancers were gone, too.

When Maurice Joyant asked Lautrec to go along on a business trip to London, he didn't hesitate. He never missed an opportunity to cross the English Channel. No matter how rough the sea, Lautrec walked the deck of the paddle steamer like an old tar, becoming more "English" with every hour that brought him closer to London. He liked the feeling of being in another world the minute he stepped aboard the steamer. And indeed, had the Channel been far wider, it could hardly have separated two more different cultures.

Queen Victoria had been on the throne for almost sixty years, and her impact on the manners and morals of her subjects was unmistakable. There were certain things "one didn't do" in Victorian England; and if one did them anyway, "one didn't talk" about them; and if one did talk about them, it was never in public. Needless to say, Lautrec discovered people who both did and talked about the things he was interested in.

He always stayed at the Charing Cross Hotel, from which he had written his mother some years before, "I'm already in the grip of the spell arising from the London hustle and bustle. Everybody wrapped up in his business and neither man nor beast letting out a useless cry or word. The hansom cabs here have an air that would put plenty of private carriages to shame. . . . I'm going to play at 'breakfasting' and start my campaign with the National Gallery."

Visiting the National Gallery and the British Museum was certainly one of the things he did in London. He spent hours studying the paintings, especially those of Velásquez and Paolo Uccello. But on this particular trip his first concern was to arrange a meeting between his old friends James Whistler and Maurice Joyant, who had come to London specifically to meet Whistler and talk gallery business. Lautrec fixed a luncheon appointment for the three of them. It was a success from every point of view except gastronomic. He liked everything about Whistler, that American-born, London-domiciled painter, except his standards in food.

Then Lautrec took himself off to explore "his" London. He loved the Cheapside fish market, the big stores and the little shops, the pubs and the people in them—those silent, serious drinkers who let nothing deter them from the business at hand. He always poked his head into the Liberty shop to see what was new in printed fabrics. What he especially liked, though, were the hours he spent tapping his way through the hundreds of small alleys and bypaths of old London. They reminded him of Montmartre.

Adding to Lautrec's pleasures on this trip was Charles Conder, a man eminently equipped for the job of companion and guide. The English painter, after four years in Paris, was back home and more than willing to accompany his French friend around town. If there was anyone who could match Lautrec's drinking, it was Conder. Together they explored London's night life, which differed very little in kind and not at all in degree—a fact which would have surprised the Queen —from that of Paris, except that the girls spoke English. The main difference for Lautrec was that in London he was careful not to drink to excess. Queen Victoria's policemen were much rougher on public drunks than were their Parisian counterparts.

London was buzzing with scandal during this visit. The name that cropped up in every conversation was that of Oscar Wilde, celebrated writer and dramatist, the center of gravity for a whole circle of English aristocrats and intellectuals, including Conder. At the height of his powers and fame, Oscar Wilde had run afoul of British law on a morals charge. He was, it was alleged, a homosexual. His trial was coming up that very week and nobody talked about anything else.

Lautrec felt no great sympathy for either the man or his writing; they were too mannered and artificial for his tastes. He was, however, outraged at the intrusion of law into a man's private life. The all-tolerant painter felt strongly about every man's right to his own destiny, and asked Conder to take him to meet Oscar Wilde.

It was a long and wordy visit. The man who dominated the conversation was less a host than a performer. Fascinated by Wilde's appearance, Lautrec asked him to pose. The writer arrogantly refused. But there was nothing to stop the painter's eye and memory from functioning, nothing to keep him from observing every expression on the large face, every shift in the massive body. Back at the Charing Cross Hotel, he made sketch after sketch. There would be time enough in Montmartre for the actual portrait.

Lautrec divided the rest of his stay in London between attending the trial of Oscar Wilde in the Old Bailey courthouse, eating porterhouse steaks at the Criterion and Horse Shoe Restaurants, and pondering the English. For once he was almost sober.

To Maurice Guibert one could say "Let's be off!" and feel certain that he'd pack his bags immediately. Guibert's capacity for drink and amusement met Lautrec's requirements. He was one of "the little tyrant's" devoted slaves. Maxime Dethomas was another. As soon as Lautrec had finished Wilde's portrait he persuaded his two friends to go with him for a holiday at the seashore. They went to Granville on the Brittany coast, with Lautrec wearing a yachtsman's cap and blue pea jacket with gold buttons.

He was an excellent swimmer. Once in the water, the

body in the droopy bathing suit no longer looked deformed. The head, arms, and shoulders one saw could have belonged to a small athlete. The legs were no more visible than those of a swan sailing majestically over the water. Getting in and out of the water could be embarrassing, but by now Lautrec was used to children who pointed and adults who laughed. With that capacity of his for self-caricature, he would strike heroic poses on the beach and ask Guibert to photograph him. When the time came to go, he hated to leave.

Lautrec had promised to spend part of his holiday with his family in the Midi. Why not go to Le Havre and take a boat down the coast of France, instead of the dreary train ride from Paris? Why not take his friends with him? Dethomas couldn't go; he had work to do in Paris; but Guibert agreed.

As soon as the two of them arrived in Le Havre, Lautrec headed for the port. He was a longtime client in the bars that lined the waterfront. Located for the convenience of thirsty sailors, those bars were the nearest you could get in France to a pub. The English barmaids who presided over them, young and not so young, wore prim black dresses, little white aprons, and stiff, starched collars. Lautrec's favorite was Miss Dolly, the soul of the Star, and he filled pages of his sketch pad with her. Then, fortified by Miss Dolly's beer, he took Guibert on a tour of the waterfront to look for a ship heading south.

Since the long-ago days in Nice when he was recovering from his first fall, Lautrec had been fascinated by sailors and the life of the sea. He knew the coast of France as well as he knew the alleys of Montmartre. He knew most of the ships that sailed down it, too, and when he spotted the steamer *Chili* riding at anchor, he was delighted. The *Chili* was an old friend. It was bound for Africa, going along the coast of France. Its captain, chief mechanic, and entire crew greeted Lautrec like a blood brother. Their enthusiastic welcome stemmed partly from anticipation of the gastronomic orgy in store.

Lautrec and the *Chili* already had their traditions. He made his purchases before boarding: cases of wine and port, olive oil, fresh herbs, spices. A few hours out of Le Havre the *Chili* stopped off the coast of Brittany to buy fresh lobsters and other seafood from the fishing boats plying the waters. Then Lautrec took possession of the galley. He worked hard, producing lobster *à l'Armoricaine* and other specialties from his own secret recipes. That the *Chili* would not reach Bordeaux, its first stop, at the prescribed hour was a foregone conclusion; but by then all hands on board had eaten and drunk so royally that for them time ceased to exist.

The painter-turned-chef hardly emerged from the galley all the way from Le Havre to Bordeaux. Otherwise, he might have noticed the red-haired passenger in Cabin 54 sooner. Once having seen her, he refused categorically to disembark at Bordeaux. Wherever the *Chili* took her he would go, too.

Even for Guibert, accustomed as he was to "the little

The *Passenger in Cabin 54* became the subject of one of Lautrec's finest posters; 23¼″ x 15¾″, 1896.

tyrant's" whims and fancies, this was going a bit far. The *Chili*'s next stop was Lisbon.

The passenger in Cabin 54 (Lautrec never did learn her name) was a pretty young thing on her way to Dakar to join her husband at the French consulate. She was very shy and very soulful, and she spent most of her time aboard the *Chili* in a deck chair staring out into space. Not once did Lautrec speak to her. He merely devoured her with his eyes from a discreet distance and sketched.

At Lisbon he wanted to continue on to Dakar, but this time Guibert put his foot down. Enough was enough— even for a redhead. Lautrec had to resign himself to putting this girl of his fleeting dream on paper.

15

IN JANUARY, 1896, Joyant opened a one-man exhibit of Lautrec's works in Paris. It was one of the most controversial shows ever held in the capital, and it came at a bad time. By now, at thirty-two, the painter had produced an astonishing number of paintings and lithographs, including many executed in brothels, which would have profoundly shocked the average Parisian. Worse, they could get him into serious trouble with the law.

Some six years earlier, a certain Senator Bérenger had had a law passed against immorality in window displays. Having won his first skirmish with the devil, "Old Man Decency," as he was known to the irreverent, then went after posters. So thunderingly did he rail against indecent murals that some wit composed a song to explain sin: "Blame it on the posters." In this same year of 1896 a public-spirited group organized a League for the Moralization of the Masses, and the battle lines were drawn. While the moralists polished their sermons, the journalists sharpened their pencils.

It was not a good time to be exhibiting pictures of "the girls." To make sure that the average Parisian didn't see Lautrec's, Joyant arranged to hang the more daring ones in two locked rooms above the gallery. Included in the upstairs exhibit were the studies Lautrec had made for an album on women in brothels, as well as the ten lithographs for the album *Elles*.

There was also a painting of two lesbians, called simply *The Friends*, a subject Lautrec treated with complete candor and naturalness. To him there was nothing shocking in the *Woman in a Corset*, or the *Woman at Her Toilette*; nothing unnatural in his drawing of a young girl in bed, receiving a visit from an older woman in a chemise. To anyone raising an eyebrow he might have replied, "I paint what I see." He had repaid his subjects' lack of inhibition with friendliness and understanding and painted them as he would any other women. The only difference was that he knew them better. "Models," he once told Thadée Natanson, "are like stuffed animals; these girls are alive."

In fact, it was their very aliveness that would have outraged Senator Bérenger. With "Old Man Decency" in mind, Joyant and Lautrec paid careful attention to which pictures they hung in the gallery downstairs. They locked the two rooms upstairs, and to make sure

Salon in Rue des Moulins, by Henri de Toulouse-Lautrec.
Oil painting, 43″ x 47″, 1894.

it stayed locked, Lautrec kept the key in his pocket along with the crayons, toothbrushes, grater, and nutmeg.

The only people privileged to climb the stairs were critics, connoisseurs, and collectors. The rooms to which they were admitted were in themselves worth seeing: strawberry velvet drapes, green curtains, pale-yellow furniture. But what caused the comments were the drawings, paintings, and lithographs that covered the walls. Naturally, when word got around, the gallery was thronged. Everybody wanted to go upstairs, but the painter was adamant. To art dealers he said "Nothing for sale." To everybody else he refused admission. It was bad enough dealing with the art critics.

"Cynicism!" "Obscenity!" Such were the reactions of many of them. So many, in fact, that Lautrec's friend Gustave Geoffroy was moved to write an impassioned article. "It is impossible for me to have such an impression," he said. "The search for truth is the concern of the maestro, stronger than all the curiosities and all the intentions of those who view."

The article became more and more vehement as it continued. "Lautrec has created terrifying works," Geoffroy wrote, "throwing the harshest light on one of the hells of misery and vice that lurk behind our façade of civilization." He wrote about the "naïve-featured women" whose lives might have been happier, had society been less indifferent. Carried away, he attributed motives to Lautrec which must have taken the painter by surprise.

As was to be expected, Geoffroy's eloquence brought even greater crowds to the gallery. Among them was Isaac de Camondo, a wealthy banker and collector, who was one of the privileged few admitted to the inner sanctum. The portrait of *Cha-U-Kao the Female Clown* that hangs in the Louvre today is the one that de Camondo bought (at the unheard-of price of one thousand francs) and later donated to the museum. Nevertheless, the painter remained chary with his key, and not many people climbed the stairs to the green-curtained rooms.

Ordinarily, Lautrec would have scorned public criticism (accustomed as he was to that of his family), but there was a strange moral climate to the times. The Victorian English weren't the only people equating "vice" with the end of the century. It seemed that the more rapidly changes occurred, the more rabidly some people opposed them.

Senator Bérenger's campaign had begun with posters; now it gained momentum. In the same city where scientists like Louis Pasteur and Marie Curie were opening some people's minds, the tempo of change was closing others. Women wearing trousers! And now, complained scandalized citizens, some women when they climbed aboard those electric tramways even displayed their ankles. The bolder ones went so far as to wear embroidered stockings.

The Church filled the Sunday air with stern warnings to the people. Provincial mayors, thankful that their youth was saved from the wicked capital, vigilantly maintained decency. One mayor indignantly returned a marble statue donated by a wealthy citizen for the public garden when he discovered it was of a nude woman.

Lautrec was right to keep the upstairs rooms locked.

"Only in the country one regrets being a bachelor," Lautrec once wrote to his mother. That had been years before, when he was visiting the Greniers at their summer cottage. The thought came to him again as he was sprawling on the grass, watching Misia Natanson move like a queen among her guests. He listened for her laugh. He remarked the flush of her cheeks, how her hair curled from the excitement or the heat, or both. Then, never one to yearn for the unattainable, he stretched out and went to sleep.

He slept a good deal these days. Overwork, on top of the usual alcoholic rounds, had exhausted him. Seeing him one day at the *Revue Blanche*, looking pale and worn out, Thadée Natanson had urged him to come out to their country place in Villeneuve-sur-Yonne for a few weeks.

The Natansons' house on the river Yonne had once been a relay station for horses and travelers on their dusty journeys to or from Paris. They still called it "*le Relais*," but now it was a relay station for the *Revue Blanche*. It was as comfortable and casual as its owners, who filled it with guests. Everybody came, went, and did as he pleased.

The painters Bonnard and Vuillard set up their easels in the garden. Mallarmé, when he wasn't reciting poetry to Misia, was composing it. Romain Coolus, Tristan Bernard, and the others from the *Revue Blanche* (the group frequently included Gabriel Tapié de Céleyran, who trailed his cousin like a shadow) spent their time talking. Having disposed of Senator Bérenger and Morality in a few sentences, they went on to more burning issues.

Lautrec rowed and swam, painted and read, and spent blissful hours watching Misia or listening to her play the piano. Occasionally he joined the discussion. Whatever the topic, Lautrec never lacked for pithy comment, delivered in his own inimitable style—a mixture of Paris slang, Midi dialect, and Lautrec word inventions, gustily uttered, with a ghost of a lisp. His friends had rarely seen him like this, so relaxed and rested. And so sober.

Purposely, the Natansons served no alcohol between meals. At the table, to everybody's surprise, Lautrec drank very little more wine than the others. But the secret of his sobriety by day was revealed late one night, when Thadée Natanson caught him sneaking in through the garden gate after a visit to the village café. Alcohol, even the limited variety provided by a backwoods café, had become as essential as breathing.

It was clear now that by drinking Lautrec was able to forget. Sometimes his friends were afraid to let him go home alone after a night in the bars—not because he was drunk, but because he wasn't drunk enough.

Thadée helped his friend get to bed and then lay awake himself for hours. One particular occasion kept haunting him. It had happened in the wee hours of the morning, when only a few drinkers were still left after the night's rounds. As they stood on the corner waiting for cabs, Lautrec kept shifting from one foot to another, fiddling with his cane, not saying a word. One of the women in the party went over to him and started to talk. She kept insisting that he come to lunch at her apartment the next day. The more he refused the more she insisted, telling him that she had a surprise for him, not taking no for an answer. He finally agreed, and they put him in a cab.

On the way home the others asked her why she had been so insistent about the luncheon appointment. "What do you want?" she replied. "Seeing him there so sad, so mortally sad, I was afraid to leave him alone . . . I felt that it was necessary to give him, at all costs, a reason to stay alive until tomorrow noon."

Knowing Lautrec as they did, the people who received his lithographed invitation were more amused than surprised. It read: "Henri de Toulouse-Lautrec will be greatly honored if you will take a cup of milk with him on Saturday, May 15 [1897], at about half-past three in the afternoon." The drawing which accompanied the invitation showed his small person got up as a lion tamer, with spurs and whip, fearlessly facing a cow with a bulging udder.

"Milk" was a very snobbish word just then. A fancy

dairy, in order to inaugurate its new shop and launch its products, had plastered the walls of Paris with a poster proclaiming that "A good glass of milk is better than a glass of wine." The city's fashionable, dressed to the hilt, hurried to the opening. With squeals of delight they tasted the milk and cream which up until now they would have considered bad for the liver if not downright poisonous. Those fortunate enough to have a personal invitation took home a small pot of butter as a souvenir.

Lautrec, who couldn't resist taking potshots at snobs whenever possible, had found the ideal occasion. He was having a housewarming; "a milk party" was just the thing.

The painter had moved again. His new apartment was on the avenue Frochot, very close to his mother's place on the rue de Douai, where he would now be able to drop in for meals. This alone would have pleased Countess Adèle, even had her son's letter been less ecstatic: "I have finally found . . . an extraordinary apartment. I hope to end my days in peace there. There's a country-sized kitchen, trees, and nine windows giving out on gardens. It's the whole top floor of a little house next to the Dihaus'; we will be able to have musical evenings."

The Dihaus were musician friends of the family who had often played for Lautrec and sat for portraits, but at the moment they were not his first order of business. First would come the housewarming, as soon as his new furniture arrived. As usual, he had gone to Brussels to look around for the latest fashions. He bought low couches and covered them with cushions, the newest style. He also ordered, according to Joyant, who was greatly impressed, "a limewood fireplace set in green and yellow tiles, and a table made of natural ash, fitted with a handle by which it could be raised or lowered to suit the guests."

The apartment consisted of one large, bright room with a narrow, very steep interior staircase leading to two small rooms above. One was his bedroom, the other his dressing room. There was the usual profusion of easels, canvases, chairs, rowing machine, and small tables below. A new acquisition was a huge wicker armchair, in which his friend Paul Leclercq, one of the founders of the *Revue Blanche,* sat for his portrait.

Leclercq couldn't believe his eyes. The apartment made such an impression on him that years later he could still recall its details. What he particularly remembered was the table in Lautrec's dressing room. It was cluttered with enormous nail files and sponges of all dimensions. There were fancy soaps that gave off a delicate scent of butter and almonds, plus a special short-handled brush for lathering his body. But mostly there were hairbrushes—dozens of them.

Like father, like son. Both Alphonse and Henri went to excesses when the fancy took them. Not one brush, but dozens. And not merely a housewarming party, but an event.

Where father and son differed was in the importance

each attached to public opinion. Though Count Alphonse arrogantly flouted his own eccentricities, he was jealous of the family name. Alphonse was not at all pleased when a tongue-in-cheek article appeared in *La Vie Parisienne* a few days after his son's housewarming. Henri was unperturbed.

"Under the pretext of showing them his recent pictures and drawings," the snide journalist had written, "one of your youngest masters invited his friends this week to a cup of milk in his studio. A large 'art nouveau' table held cups of milk, cream cheeses, and strawberries. . . . Straw-bottomed chairs surrounded the table, the walls were hung with mats, there were wild flowers in profusion. . . . A smart barman in well-starched white jacket and trousers stood in a recess, discreetly preparing cocktails, to which the male guests, frock-coated and with flowers in their buttonholes, did honor, leaving the ladies to enjoy the picnic fare which was too spartan for them."

Measured by all standards except those of Count Alphonse and the Jockey Club, the party was a success. So was its host. Henri de Toulouse-Lautrec was the painter with the sharpest pencil on Montmartre, the most devoted entourage, and the loudest critics. The year 1897 was a high point. It was also a turning point.

16

LIFE WAS STILL beautiful, but it was beginning to have its gray moments. His friends noticed growing patches of clouds in Lautrec's usual optimism, and even in his ardor for work. Dropping in one day at the new apartment, François Gauzi was alarmed to find dust on the easel. Paul Leclercq sat less frequently in the wicker armchair for his portrait and more often at the bar, keeping an eye on his friend. The little man who loved to laugh and had always been the first with a quip was becoming silent and irritable. He was tired, unable to work, afraid to be alone and yet short-tempered in company. At thirty-three, Lautrec looked much older than his years.

Dr. Bourges ordered an immediate holiday. Enlisting the help of other devoted friends, he persuaded Lautrec to forgo temporarily the "night cups" and "rainbow cups" of the bar on the rue Royale and accompany Maurice Joyant to the sea.

They went to Crotoy on the Bay of Somme, where Joyant owned a fishing boat. Slowly, in the tiny fishing village where the proprietor of the café had never heard of gin-whiskey, Lautrec began to relax. The bite of the wind and the strong odor of the sea replaced the city smells of smoke, alcohol, and unaired beds. The tides dictated his rounds.

The leathery old sea dog who operated Joyant's boat found nothing strange in the man who eyed him so gravely, always sketching, never saying a word. Silence was appreciated in Crotoy; talking scared away the fish.

Fortunately, the weather was fine. The two Paris-pale sophisticates soon looked like the sunbaked fishermen around them. They spent their days fishing, sailing, duck hunting, or just lying on deck in the sun. The watchful, faithful Joyant saw to it that the supply of alcohol on board was rationed. And if Lautrec wound up at the bar in the evening, it wasn't for long; closing time came early in Crotoy. After a few weeks he was ready to return to Paris.

Now it was Maxime Dethomas who persuaded him to prolong his holiday. They went to Holland for a leisurely trip through the canals, including just enough stopovers in towns along the way to take the edge off the painter's thirst. A detour brought them to Haarlem, the city where Frans Hals had painted most of his master-pieces. But Lautrec was no longer the same man who only a few years before had written his mother so enthusiastically about a trip to Amsterdam with Anquetin. He had lived too hard since then. He soon tired of wandering "Baedeker in hand among the Dutch masters."

One day, walking on the quay, Lautrec turned to see a band of urchins waddling along behind, imitating his limp and banging sticks on the cobblestones. He told Dethomas he was going home. In Paris everybody knew him. Besides, it was time to go back to work.

The unfinished portrait of Paul Leclercq was just as he had left it: on an easel covered with dust. Quickly, with the sureness born of acute observation and a lifetime of work, Lautrec added the finishing touches and then went on to spend the rest of the summer with the Natansons at Villeneuve-sur-Yonne.

One of the painter's favorite pastimes at the Natansons' was to explore the attic under the roof, filled with a collection of relics whose origin nobody knew. There were trunks, boxes, and piles of old journals and newspapers: the record left behind by generations of travelers who had stopped off at the Relais to rest and wash up. Sometimes hours would go by before Lautrec emerged from the attic, with wisps of cobweb still in his beard. Once he dressed in a hoopskirt and ruffled sleeves, in the role of a woman who had told her husband she couldn't travel one step farther. Another time he was the weary husband himself, in cocked hat and breeches. In his hand Lautrec would be waving his newest tidbit: a page torn out of an old fashion book, or a spicy item from a long-forgotten scandal sheet.

Misia Natanson, dressed in delicious pastels and looking like something plucked from the garden, flitted in and out of his hours. He listened while she played the piano. He stroked her bare feet with a feather while she sat reading under a tree. Or he went into the kitchen to prepare a special sauce for her dinner. Vuillard caught him there one day and put on canvas what he saw: an endearing little man in yellow pants and red shirt, the familiar felt hat pulled over his forehead.

His friends would never forget Lautrec's remark: "When one says he doesn't give a damn, it's because he does." It revealed that even with those who loved him, he sometimes found it hard to snap his fingers at fate. No matter how well-meaning human beings were, they could be thoughtless. Animals, never.

Lautrec loved animals almost as much as he loved people, and in fact made little distinction between them. His caricatures often took the form of animals; his animals were as individual as people. This man from Albi, who had grown up among creatures who crawled, galloped, trotted, wriggled, and flew, took to going almost every day to the Paris zoo. Usually Leclercq went along.

From the stables near his house, owned by one Edmond Calmèse, Lautrec rented Philibert, a pony which he lavishly spoiled, and a small carriage. Then, swinging by the Champs Elysées to pick up Leclercq, he would head for the zoo. Each day was like a homecoming, and he had his favorites.

The giant anteater, who would hardly win beauty prizes, was one of them. The creature positively capered for joy when it saw Lautrec approaching. For as long as an hour at a time, the painter would sit in front of its cage on a folding stool and exchange affectionate greetings with a friend who happened to be an anteater. The armadillo, the llama, the parakeets and pelicans, the apes, all were his friends.

Lautrec had an almost intuitive knowledge of how animals behaved. He had been drawing them all his life; never once did he make them ridiculous. Between him and the animal world there was mutual respect and understanding. Now, at Joyant's suggestion, he began illustrating *Histoires Naturelles* ("Natural Histories"), written by Jules Renard.

Like Renard's descriptions, Lautrec's illustrations for *Histoires Naturelles* go far beyond "animal studies." They are portraits. There is no doubt that the donkey he drew knew the deliveryman's route by heart, and was resigned to plodding it. The painter probed as deeply under fur and hide as he did under human skin for what lay buried underneath.

Philibert could have found his way alone to the zoo. Day after day the pony trotted down the Champs Elysées, picked up Leclercq, and deposited the two men in front of the anteater. Had that been the only place he took them, Countess Adèle would have rejoiced. Unfortunately, Philibert also knew the way to every café in the park. It happened more and more frequently that when

Henri went to dine with his mother, even after a visit to the zoo, he was drunk.

At Countess Adèle's urging, Joyant had arranged a one-man show for her son in London. Anything to get Henri out of Paris! Reluctantly, the painter agreed to go on ahead to see personally to the hanging of his pictures, with the understanding that Joyant would join him before the exhibit opened. Alone in London, Lautrec was wondering why he had let them talk him into it.

The manager of the Charing Cross Hotel had greeted the Frenchman like an old friend. Everything was the same—his room, the chambermaid, the bootblack, the English breakfast, and the scones at teatime. Only he had changed. On his first walk through the city he knew so well, he lost his way and was terrified.

The traffic in London was even worse than in Paris. Whereas the year before he had counted perhaps one automobile for every thirty hansoms, the proportion was now one to twenty. Like Parisians, Londoners were forever dodging and ducking, and like their counterparts across the Channel they shook their heads over what would happen if things continued. The difference was that the English muttered to themselves, while the French ranted out loud. Londoners did almost everything more privately, including drinking.

That was the trouble. Ever since his first visit, when he had seen an English "bobby" give short treatment to a well-dressed, middle-aged drunk, Lautrec was afraid to go out in the British capital. Back in his hotel room alone, he was suddenly seized by the fears that came these days in suffocating waves. Only drinking would make them go away, or sleeping—when he could sleep. That, too, was frightening. Often he fell asleep at the table, in the middle of a conversation or riding in the carriage. Nights he lay agonizingly awake. Worst of all was to be alone.

Each morning he went first to the gallery to see how things were going and then to the railroad station to meet the train arriving from Dover. Perhaps someone he knew would get off. Someone from home. When Maurice Joyant finally arrived, Lautrec's joy was like that of a small child lost in the park who has found his mother at last.

The London exhibit, despite the fact that the Prince of Wales attended the opening, was not a success. By the time the doors opened, Lautrec was so exhausted that he fell asleep. He was still sleeping, curled up in a chair, when the heir to the British throne arrived, to the horror of everyone but the royal guest himself. Prince Edward gallantly refused to have the painter awakened. He went around the gallery examining every painting, and even bought one—as a reminder to himself, perhaps, of more carefree days when he had sat incognito at the Moulin Rouge watching La Goulue dance. But the Victorian public was outraged both by the painter's manners and by his manner of painting. Lautrec's candid realism and his choice of subjects were unwelcome reminders to a hypocritical society of what they felt should be properly swept under the rug. For the first time that he could remember, Lautrec was glad to leave London.

"I'm relishing my avenue-Frochot tranquility so much," he wrote his mother after the homeward Channel crossing, "that the least effort is impossible for me. My painting itself is suffering, in spite of the work I must get done, and in a hurry."

It was not a good sign. He still went to the zoo every day, and he worked hard finishing up the illustrations for Jules Renard's *Histoires Naturelles*, but as 1898 drew to a close he had only fourteen paintings and a few lithographs to show for a year's work. The canvases he might have painted had been washed away in alcohol.

The New Year's Eve that was approaching had a strange, fatalistic quality to it, a sort of "what will be, will be" feeling. The world was changing so quickly that before one had digested yesterday, tomorrow was already here. Already there was talk of flying machines. As for the automobile, a certain Monsieur Desgranges confidently predicted in his magazine *Auto-Vélo* that it would soon be "not only a pleasure of the rich, but an almost practical object of utility."

The working class clamored for a modest share of the progress. Not without difficulties and violence, they finally forced a law limiting the workday for women and children to ten hours. Scandals rocked the government, anarchists bombed buildings, schoolmasters argued among themselves over whether there was too much or too little education for the masses.

In the worrisome and lengthening days of December, Paris prepared to celebrate New Year's Eve. There was a grim determination in the capital to make the most of the occasion. While cabarets laid in mountains of oysters and champagne, neighborhood cafés stocked up on cheap wine and beer. Come what may, everybody prepared to drink a toast to the future.

The old century had only one more year to run—and Lautrec not many more.

17

"PEOPLE" WERE AFTER HIM. The only place he felt safe was in Edmond Calmèse's stable, where Philibert rubbed his warm nose against him and the smell of hay brought back memories of the Château du Bosc. Nobody could get at him there among the harnesses and saddles.

Last night "they" had tried to break into his apartment. At one o'clock in the morning he had had to wake up the wine merchant across the way and ask him to send over his son to search for "them." "They" even followed him on the street, in broad daylight, and of what use was his little cane then? It could only protect him in bed, against the microbes and strange flying insects that infested his room.

That was how he had burned his hand. He had to keep the fire going all the time in the stove to keep "the bugs" away. Everybody was out to get him. Even his cousin Gabriel was a spy; he was as much against him as all the rest. Even his mother. Why wasn't she in Paris? What was a sick grandmother compared to him?

He must remind Calmèse that they were out of wine. Good old Calmèse; he was the only one of the lot who knew how to drink. Mustn't forget the wine. And the handkerchiefs. What did he want handkerchiefs for? Oh yes, to wrap around his hand. Better tell old Berthe he needed clean handkerchiefs. Was it today he promised to go to the rue de Douai for lunch? Lunch? Or was it dinner? There "they" were again. The best thing would be to spray his room with kerosene. Calmèse must have some wine stashed away. He'd better go now; they'd be coming any minute.

Hallucinations. Nightmares. Panic. Lautrec was desperately sick. Alcohol had done its job.

Poor old Berthe Sarrazin was at her wit's end. When the news was too bad she didn't dare write to Countess Adèle, who had left her behind in the apartment on the rue de Douai to look after Monsieur Henri. She wrote to Adeline instead, the faithful old servant who had brought up Monsieur Henri at the Château du Bosc.

"Everybody is amazed that he can keep up such a life," she wrote to Adeline. "It would be better if poor Madame doesn't know about it. Now then, Adeline, it's an act of charity to keep her in the dark. What can one do? There's nothing to do but wait till he drops, which perhaps will happen before long. You ask me if he's working. He doesn't do a stroke any more."

Lautrec was often ill during this period. This undated photograph shows the artist sleeping.

Which wasn't altogether true. Just after New Year's Eve, Jane Avril, the ever-faithful, had asked him to do a poster for her. He had shown her standing in a graceful pose with snakes twined around her body, a first-rate poster, one of his best. "They" had rejected it. He began varnishing his other paintings with glycerine to keep them safe. He had to use an old sock to rub them down; he was out of handkerchiefs. Sometimes he used petroleum jelly and glycerine on his pictures.

"I'm very much afraid he's going to ruin them all," Berthe wrote to Countess Adèle. "But he doesn't touch the fire any more. . . . This morning I gave him eight pocket handkerchiefs."

Berthe did her best to cheer up Madame and keep watch over Monsieur Henri. "I'm staying as long as possible at his place. He talks and talks and he doesn't go out. He forgets to drink. If one could be with him all the time to keep him busy perhaps he wouldn't think about drinking any more."

But Lautrec continued to get worse. Countess Adèle hired a male nurse to look after him, but the poor man was no match for her son. With the help of Calmèse, an alcoholic as confirmed as himself, Henri managed to squander vast sums of money at the wine merchant's and the neighborhood bar and on the unsavory characters who hovered around him, an easily recognized prey. What he didn't spend, he gave away. Even his bed pillow ended up in Calmèse's apartment.

"That pig Calmèse, they should put him in jail. He's

going to be the death of poor Monsieur," Berthe wrote.

Poor Berthe worried constantly about the characters who followed Monsieur Henri like vultures. Though the burglars he was frightened of were imaginary, the thefts that took place were real enough. His watch disappeared, his good tiepin, the beautiful new scarf he had bought not long ago. Unscrupulous shopkeepers sold him all kinds of junk at scandalous prices. He was constantly looking for money, either to give away or to spend on alcohol. Somewhere he acquired a puppy—Pamela, he called it—for which he bought a nursing bottle; now Berthe had that, too, on top of everything else. She poured out her heart to Adeline:

"I don't know what to tell you. It's still the same old thing. Monsieur keeps on drinking and now and then becomes disagreeable. Monsieur Mallet [a doctor] says he thinks he's better, but as for me, I don't think so. For two nights now I don't know where he has been sleeping. . . . How will it all end, my poor Adeline?"

The night grew darker and darker, the rages of temper more violent. Now he hardly ate at all, just drank. The time came at last when Countess Adèle had to commit her son for care. At the beginning of March 1899, Henri de Toulouse-Lautrec entered a clinic in Neuilly for detoxification.

The Saint-James Clinic had known other days. The elegantly gowned ladies and gentlemen who had strolled through its beautiful gardens a century before had been guests of the aristocratic owners of a splendid villa. Those who walked along its shaded paths today, accompanied by nurses and guardians, were in varying degrees mentally ill. The only thing they had in common with their forebears was wealth, for to be treated in these luxurious surroundings was enormously expensive. Damasked chairs and sofas still graced the drawing rooms; some of the patients had three-room apartments and their own private gardens. But the gates to the outside were locked.

When the fog lifted and Lautrec realized where he was, he was oppressed by a new terror: the anguish of one who is trapped. He was not mad. As the alcohol left his system, lucidity returned—and with it memory and perception. The two small rooms with grilled doors, at the end of a dimly lit narrow corridor, were as restraining as the cage of the anteater. The male nurse who occupied the room next to his was a keeper. He saw himself through the distorting mirror of a freak house, reflected in the bizarre behavior of the people around him. Not even a lifetime of being different could soften the shock.

Nevertheless, Lautrec's recovery was rapid. By March 12, Countess Adèle was already able to drop Maurice Joyant a note: "He reads and amuses himself a bit by drawing." Three days later Joyant went, with heavy heart, to visit his friend in the clinic.

"I shall always remember my first visit to Lautrec," Joyant recorded, "and my anguished sadness . . . Lautrec—lucid, calm, already at work with pencil and sketches—greeted me like a liberator, a link to the outside world, but filled with fear that, through family and medical complicity, charitable or interested, he might be eternally enclosed there."

The painter looked thin and drawn, his skin yellow, but the glaze was gone from his eyes. Though his hands still trembled, his vision was as clear as ever. The garden in which the two friends walked, with its spring bulbs about to burst into color, might have been the Bois de Boulogne, but for the other strollers they met, each with his white-uniformed attendant. Lautrec turned to Joyant and whispered, "Help me!"

Yet he knew that only one thing could help him. Two days after the visit he wrote Joyant a letter, asking him to send watercolor paints, including sepia, and some brushes, India ink, paper, and lithographic crayons and stones. Only work would liberate him from the clinic just as, when he was fifteen years old, it had freed him from his crutches. Lautrec began to draw again. He conceived a plan and enlisted Joyant's help.

Meanwhile, his absence from his usual haunts had been noticed—not by his friends, who knew where he was, but by his critics. With no marked concern for the facts, they rushed into print.

"It was bound to end like this," Parisians read in *Le Journal* over their morning *café au lait*. "Toulouse-Lautrec was making straight for a clinic. He has been shut up, and now madness, tearing off its mask, will place its official signature on the paintings, drawings, and posters in which it has so long been anonymously present."

The *Echo de Paris* told its readers they would be "wrong to pity Lautrec; he is rather to be envied. . . . The only place where happiness is to be found nowadays is a padded cell in a lunatic asylum." Among the more flattering things the article called him was "a hunchbacked Don Juan."

Joyant made certain that Lautrec didn't read what was being written about him. He wanted nothing to disturb the painter in his self-appointed task. Lautrec had undertaken to produce, with Joyant as editor, a complete album of drawings about the circus—entirely from memory. This, at a time when his detractors were portraying him in a straitjacket.

The slander, the rumors, and the gossip continued. To put an end to them, the faithful Joyant persuaded Arsène Alexandre, art critic of the *Le Figaro Illustré*, to visit the clinic. If the article Alexandre wrote, entitled "A Cure," couldn't silence Lautrec's enemies, it would at least reassure his friends:

"I have just seen a madman who is full of wisdom, a drunkard who has stopped drinking, a man described as done for, but who never looked better. . . . This 'doomed' man has such intense vitality, this so-called abortion possesses such reserves of strength, that those who watched him plunging to his ruin discover to their amazement that he is now a new man."

Not quite. The "new man" was suffering tortures. Not to drink! There were times when Lautrec thought he really would go mad. He wrote to Berthe: "I beg you to come to 16 avenue de Madrid in the morning and bring me a pound of good ground coffee. Also bring me a bottle of rum. Bring me the whole lot in a locked valise, and ask to speak to me."

"I've just seen Monsieur Henri," Berthe wrote Countess Adèle after her visit. "He is still the same, if anything better, above all very calm. He received me nicely and was glad to see me. . . . I brought some coffee, the chocolate drops, and the handkerchiefs. . . . I didn't bring the rum, as Madame can well imagine, but I told Monsieur that I had brought some but that the doorkeeper took it away from me when I came in."

Lautrec advised Berthe to remove the bottle from the doorkeeper on her way out, since the latter would surely drink it—and add insult to injury by claiming it was to *his* health. He still had his sense of humor, fortunately. But the strain of abstinence was almost unbearable. In desperation he asked for fruit-flavored Eau Muscovite, a soft drink. "It's harmless and very refreshing. I'll drink it *gladly.*"

The good Berthe came almost every day, bringing whatever he requested so long as it wasn't alcoholic: lavender water, chocolate, coffee, biscuits, powdered cinnamon, lime juice—even Pamela the dog. "She recognized him right away," Berthe wrote, "and couldn't make enough fuss over him."

He had other visitors, too. Misia came. If he was embarrassed to see her under such circumstances, he concealed it. He referred to his current residence as "Saint-James *Plage*" ("beach"); sometimes he called it "Madrid-les-Bains," as though it were one more of the fashionable watering places which had punctuated his youth.

Daily the pile of circus drawings grew higher. Early in April two eminent psychiatrists came to see their notorious patient. They found that he "manifested at no time any signs of emotional anxiety, nor excitation, nor intellectual depression." Furthermore, the doctors continued, "a very thorough examination revealed none of the signs of delirium mentioned in our previous report." And if loss of memory was one of the disturbing symptoms that had landed Lautrec in a mental hospital, he was well on his way to demonstrating that he had recovered total recall.

"When I have made a certain number of drawings, they won't be able to keep me here." This was what he had said to Joyant that day in the garden. He had worked without respite ever since. From the profundities of his memory he produced clowns, acrobats, liontamers, dancers, and equestrians, drawn with incredible precision and verve. The doctors didn't have to be connoisseurs to know that what they saw were works of art.

Now he was allowed to leave the avenue de Madrid every day, though not unaccompanied. Instead of Leclercq, the nurse from the clinic stood beside him in front of the cages at the zoo. They went for long walks and, most important of all, Lautrec was able to visit Joyant in his gallery again and to buy the art supplies he needed.

He produced thirty-nine major works on the circus during his confinement in the Saint-James Clinic. They all have a single trait in common which strikes one as curious: the benches around the ring are empty; there are no spectators. Was it merely that he wanted to concentrate on the performers, so vigorously evoked through sheer memory? Or did he purposely eliminate the audience? Perhaps he himself had had too many onlookers during these past months.

"I have bought my liberty with my drawings," he exulted to Joyant. On May 17, 1899, Toulouse-Lautrec returned home to the avenue Frochot.

Countess Adèle wasn't taking any chances. On the advice of the clinic doctors, she engaged a "companion" for her son, whose chief responsibility was to keep Henri from drinking. Prudently, she chose a man with a bad stomach: Monsieur Viaud, unable to tolerate alcohol, never touched a drop of liquor. But that wasn't his only qualification for the job.

Paul Viaud was a distant relative of the family. He happened also to be unattached, in financial difficulties, and available. But above all, he was tactful, discreet, pleasant, affable—and genuinely devoted to Lautrec. Otherwise he never could have fulfilled his duties.

Monsieur Viaud and Lautrec carried out their respective roles with tacit understanding. Lautrec sometimes introduced his companion as "M'sieu Viaud, my mentor," but more often he was simply "My friend, M'sieu Viaud." People rarely saw one without the other. Where the painter went, the watchdog followed—those were the rules of the game.

M'sieu Viaud had his baptism of fire at the party Lautrec gave in his studio to celebrate his return to the world. In introducing his new "friend," whose function all the guests knew, the host was the least embarrassed person in the room. He was the only one who referred to "Saint-James Plage," with the naturalness of a man just returned from vacation. Still, the gaiety was forced.

Thadée Natanson thought Lautrec looked older, thinner. He didn't ask questions about what was going on in town. Clearly this was not the same Lautrec who knew every bum and bistro on Montmartre, who kept the *Revue Blanche* offices in an uproar, who occupied the front-row seat at the Comédie Française, supervised Père Cotelle at the printing press, followed Jane Avril out of the Moulin Rouge, and sent roses to Marcelle Lender in her dressing room. Something of the old sparkle was gone. Was it only because M'sieu Viaud, with admirable unobtrusiveness, kept filling the painter's glass with Eau Muscovite?

A few weeks after the party, Lautrec and his mentor left for Le Havre. The plan as usual was to embark on a boat headed for the Midi, but M'sieu Viaud had not counted on the lure of the seaport. Though the drinks served in the waterfront bars were taboo, the barmaids were not. Lautrec headed straight for the Star, where the very sight of Miss Dolly made him reach for his pencil. At last. Back to work at last. He dashed off a letter to Joyant, asking him to send brushes and paints to Le Havre, and while the short stopover lengthened into weeks, he painted, swam, sailed—and painted some more.

Lautrec sent a finished portrait of Miss Dolly to Joyant with a letter asking him not to tell "the Administration," which was his code word for his family. In an attempt to control his habits, the family in Albi had set strict limits to his spending. They opened two bank accounts for him. Into one went a fixed monthly allowance. Joyant was the trustee for the other, in which he deposited the money received from the sale of pictures. Since by now his paintings fetched high prices, Lautrec didn't want the family to know the contents of the second bank account for fear that they would reduce those of the first.

Money was something he had always taken for granted. Now for the first time he found that his income was strictly limited, and the experience was both infuriating and humiliating. It was a reminder of the clinic, of which M'sieu Viaud was by no means the worst legacy. *That* amiable gentleman he had learned how to manage.

When Lautrec discovered that his mentor could handle a boat, he elevated his title. It was "Admiral Viaud" now, and the two of them made an odd-looking pair on the ship skirting the coast of France to Bordeaux. The small one with the cane clearly sang the tune to which the tall one danced. Bronzed by the sun and restored by the sea, Lautrec was on his way to recovery.

In Taussat he and "the Admiral" were either in or on the water all day. Lautrec went indoors only to sleep. It seemed that after the stranglehold of confinement he couldn't get enough of unlimited horizons. In the vastness of sea and sky his morale improved and the old zest for life returned. By autumn he was impatient to get back to Paris.

18

LAUTREC WAS LIKE an old trooper returning to the scene of action. He stopped in at Joyant's gallery every day to chat and check on sales (money was of great interest now), and went frequently to the theater. He was back in his old seat at the Moulin Rouge. Quickly he finished the portrait of Romain Coolus which he had begun the summer before at the Natansons', and once again— though no longer at dawn, thanks to Viaud—Père Cotelle pulled proofs while the painter breathed down his neck. Everybody on the Butte knew he was back. Everything was the same, almost, as before.

If only he weren't thirsty—!

The first time Viaud accompanied him to the Café Weber, Lautrec ordered a soft drink. The next time he took his nutmeg and grater with him. What harm could there be in a glass of port after five or six months of complete abstinence? Reluctantly, Viaud agreed. After the first drink, the second came naturally. Torn between vigilance and indulgence, "the Admiral" found the tightrope he walked growing ever more taut. It had been much easier to suggest Eau Muscovite on a fishing boat than in the middle of Paris.

Little by little, Lautrec began drinking again. Secretly. A happy find in an antique shop had solved the problem of how to drink without upsetting Viaud. Surely destiny had guided him to the dusty window where he had spotted the diminutive cane. It turned out to be hollow. Its silver handle unscrewed to reveal a glass tube which held exactly one pint of whatever he chose to fill it with—brandy, port, or rum; certainly nothing "fruit-flavored."

Each morning Lautrec pondered over a choice of the brushes on his dressing table. Then, armed with his double-purpose cane, he tapped his way from one activity to the next, drinking "just a little but often" en route. There was nothing the unsuspecting Viaud could do but worry. He noticed that the painter was having more difficulty walking. Was it imagination, or did his hands tremble? His too-bright eyes, his feverish activity —but then, everybody seemed more frenetic these days. Parisians were like runners with stopwatches in their hands.

The city was already preparing for its colossal Exposition of 1900 like a household turning itself inside out for a wedding. Workers hurrying home for lunch with unwrapped *baguettes* under their arms (the French were the biggest bread eaters in the world) watched a fantasy world grow before their eyes. The giant Ferris wheel which would be the landmark of this exposition, as the Eiffel Tower was of the last, rounded its silhouette higher and higher. Parisians called it "the lottery of the sky." Palaces of fantastic shape emerged from their foundations. Everything was going up—including prices.

Lautrec chafed at the Albi purse strings. He who so dearly loved to introduce his girls to caviar was constantly broke. In order to supplement the family's allowance he threw himself into work. At Joyant's urging, he tried several times to paint the portraits of fashionable ladies (who could pay handsomely), but these pampered, well-dressed women with their stilted manners and morals were not to his taste. He preferred women without pretensions, life's rejects. He soon gave up the portraits-to-order and returned to the subjects he loved.

Philibert the Pony, Jockey, At the Races, Promenade at the Moulin Rouge—these were what he drew. And sheet-music covers for his musician friend Dihau; theater programs; a poster (his last) for *La Gitane*, a current stage offering of dubious merit, whose only attraction was Marthe Mellot, the leading lady. As he had done all his life, he painted every day—until his hands began to tremble.

This happened more and more frequently. Then he would stop work, unscrew the silver handle of his cane, and take a sip from the glass tube so ingeniously concealed. The felt hat he always wore at the easel ("on account of the light," he explained) would begin to slip lower on his forehead. His eyes would close and Viaud, tiptoeing in, would find him asleep.

During the first few months after his return from the Midi Lautrec had worked with unrestrained zeal. Now he was visibly tired. It was getting harder and harder for him to climb the stairs to his bedroom. As the December nights grew longer, his strength for nocturnal wandering diminished. The cab drivers who used to settle him into the back seat of the carriage wondered what had happened to the little man whose tongue was so quick and whose tips were so generous.

Fortunately, he had his hollow cane. With its help he celebrated New Year's Eve among friends.

The painter began the new century with the last and the tenderest of his sentimental attachments. He and Louise Blouet were like two children. Like children, they understood each other and found unspoiled pleasure in simple things: a visit to the zoo, a drive in the Bois, or a boat trip on the Seine.

Louise Blouet worked in a millinery shop, sometimes as a mannequin, sometimes with a needle. It was Joyant who introduced them. It would have seemed an unlikely relationship, had not Louise sensed—as few women before her had—the little man's enormous need for affection, and the sincerity masked by sophistication. To her

Lautrec would never have to explain that "When one says he doesn't give a damn, it's because he does."

Willingly she sat for him, and the sketches that flowed from his pencil were a reminder of other days when the passion to paint outstripped all others. He finished several drawings and lithographs and an unforgettable portrait of Louise Blouet (*The Modiste*) in her world of feathers and veiling. The painting is almost like a still life. The face of the exquisite blond woman and the green-yellow blouse she is wearing emerge from the shadows and shapes that surround them—hatstands, boxes, shelves—like something one has happened on by accident. Louise is completely absorbed in her work. Her eyes are half closed; her delicate features express concentration. Lautrec has been permitted to enter her kingdom because she can trust him.

The lovely milliner brightened the painter's spring. When they were together he could still laugh, yet there was no question but that his health in general, and his legs in particular, were growing weaker. By the time the Exposition of 1900 opened its doors in April, Lautrec had to visit its vast grounds in a wheelchair.

The Exposition Universelle was a world's fair spun of dreams and illusions. It embroidered the skyline of Paris in silver domes and golden spires. One crossed the frontier between today and tomorrow on a moving platform which was a triumph of engineering. Nine different stairways gave access to this sidewalk that flowed like a river, and scores of bridges led from it to the various exhibits.

Fifty-one million visitors came. They wandered through the Palaces of the Nations—staring, feeling, touching, tasting, buying. Lautrec's favorite exhibit was the Japanese Pavilion. Each time he visited the exposition, either with Louise or with other friends, he went to see Japanese prints like those which had so influenced his own early lithographs, and the Japanese crafts he had always admired. Loyal member of the Toulouse-Lautrec clan that he was, he bought four Japanese dolls to send home to the latest batch of cousins at the Château du Bosc. But despite the wheelchair, he had to stop frequently at one of the many sidewalk cafés to rest, though he claimed it was only because of the noise.

Noisy it was. The crowds voiced their amazement in dozens of languages, with a cumulative volume that was deafening. People came in Japanese kimonos and Indian saris, in Mexican sarapes and Arab djellabahs, to gape at Tomorrow. They came again and again, stayed from morning till night, and then took their first subway ride home on the brand-new, just-opened, gleaming Métropolitain. "Métro" for short, because no one had time for long words. The future was beginning.

But for Lautrec it was nearly the end. He was really tired now. In May, much earlier than usual, he left Paris for Crotoy. The last thing he did before packing his bag was to give his hollow cane to a friend at the Café Weber. Viaud had discovered the secret.

This time Joyant went along to help Viaud keep an

eye on their friend—and because he was worried. He hadn't realized how much thinner Lautrec was until he saw him in a bathing suit. He seemed to have shrunk. The description in Jules Renard's diary ("An ear of corn about as tall as Toulouse-Lautrec") seemed hardly exaggerated. And yet once again, so strong was the spirit within the frail body, Lautrec improved with each day's sea air.

He even worked. When Joyant returned to the gallery after a few weeks, he took with him a large canvas showing *Joyant Duck Shooting*, dressed in yellow oilskins and looking like a tower of strength.

The painter and "the Admiral" went on to Le Havre, where the bars beckoned and Lautrec already anticipated the smile on Miss Dolly's face. Alas, things had changed. "Old chump," he wrote to Joyant, " the Star and the other bars are being watched by the police, so I leave for Taussat. Yours, Henri Lautrec and Co., Ltd.—and I do mean Limited."

He spent the summer in Taussat, went for the usual daily sails; why didn't he feel better?

In September he and Viaud went to visit Countess Adèle at Malromé. It was grape-harvesting time, a season he loved. His mother saw to his favorite dishes. He even started an ambitious painting intended to decorate the dining room where he sat nibbling at the delicacies he used to devour. It was a large portrait of "Admiral Viaud" wearing the uniform of a British admiral and directing the maneuvers of a sailing ship of the line. But the trouble was that he had to use a ladder to reach the canvas, and that tired his legs. At most he could work for an hour.

For the first time since he left home to become an art student in Paris, Lautrec had no desire to return to his studio in Montmartre and the life he knew there. He decided to spend the winter with Viaud in Bordeaux.

He sent his grandmother New Year's greetings. "I wish you a prosperous year," he wrote, "and from a ghost like me that counts double."

In March the painter suffered a slight stroke which left him temporarily paralyzed. Miraculously, he had recovered, but the warning was only too clear. Viaud tried his best to delay their return to Paris, but Lautrec's urgent insistence was unanswerable. Even the time it took to pack up and leave Bordeaux had made him impatient.

April was a busy month on the avenue Frochot. Housewives were scrubbing off the dirt of winter and gardeners were busy with bulbs. The sun shining on the eucalyptus trees was preparing springtime in Paris. In another few weeks the leaves that were still pale and tentative would frame Lautrec's windows in bright green, blotting out neighbors and turning his patch of Montmartre into a garden. For now, however, all the sun did was to highlight the dust on the glass panes.

Lautrec had come back to Paris to work in the time that was left. But first he wanted to see his friends.

"It was with heavy heart that we saw him after nine

months of absence," Joyant wrote, "thinner, feebler, hardly eating at all, but lucid and still full of verve at moments."

Lautrec's clothes hung on him, but he managed to laugh. He could hardly walk, but he spoke with vigor. He could even make jokes about himself. "I'm living on nux vomica, having been debarred from Bacchus and Venus," he told everybody.

All he drank these days was medicine. The hollow cane with the silver handle was a thing of the past. So were La Goulue and Jane Avril and Yvette Guilbert and Marcelle Lender and all the barmaids in Le Havre and all the girls on the rue d'Amboise and even the gentle Louise. All past. He had other things on his mind.

Some of the canvases, cardboards, wood panels, drawings, and sketches in Lautrec's studio had been buried in corners or stacked against walls for years. He dusted them off one by one and examined each carefully. The ones he didn't like he ruthlessly discarded; those that met his stern standards he signed. On the hundreds of unfinished ones he went to work, changing a line here, adding color there, eliminating any unnecessary detail which served only to blunt the message. The more he had matured as an artist, the fewer were the means he required to "say what he had to say." When he had completed his task, the June sun filtering through the leaves outside his windows fell on a scene of perfect order.

In July he propped the last canvas he would paint on

his easel. In 1899 Gabriel Tapié de Céleyran had passed his doctoral examination in medicine. Now in 1901, in a studio sadly uncluttered, Lautrec commemorated the event by painting *An Examination at the Faculty of Medicine*, showing his cousin defending his thesis before two august members of the medical faculty.

Lautrec had put his house in order. At the end of July he and Viaud left Paris for Taussat in the Midi.

The friends who came to see him off at the station were a cross section of the city he loved. Unable to participate fully in any of their worlds, Lautrec belonged to them all. What they shared was tek-nik. The tek-nik of riding, cycling, acting, writing, making love, dancing, singing, clowning; the tek-nik of doing what they did better than most people, because they worked at it. No human effort failed to interest Lautrec so long as it strove for perfection. The only thing that disgusted him was banality. Putting his head out of the train window for the last good-byes, the little man found the appropriate jargon, the ready pun for each of his friends, and then the train took him away.

A few weeks after he and Viaud arrived in Taussat, Lautrec had another paralytic stroke. This time a happy ending was too much to hope for. The body was too wasted by the disease within it; the years of feverish living demanded their price. On the twentieth of August, Countess Adèle went to get her son and bring him home to Malromé.

They had to take him to the table at mealtimes in a

wheelchair. There in the dining room was the portrait of "Admiral" Viaud, begun last fall and still unfinished. If Viaud would lift him onto the ladder, if he would hold him steady and hand him the brushes . . .

He added a few more touches to the specious admiral in his red uniform. Even when he could no longer leave his bed, he asked for pencil and notebook. Until they could no longer see anything, the luminous eyes saw everything and the pencil was compelled to record.

Henri Marie Raymond de Toulouse-Lautrec Monfa. The small figure under the sheet could have been that of a child fallen asleep. For not quite thirty-seven years he had "borne with himself" and said what he had to say, and on August 9, 1901, he died. The man who belonged so completely to his times had barely managed to turn the century with his beloved city.

Nobody ever again would paint Paris in quite the same way. No one would see Parisians with an eye so clear and unquestioning. No one would expect so little from, or give so much to, the City of Light.

Yet Lautrec was preeminently a painter of people—people who happened to live in Paris during *la belle époque* and thus partook of a unique time and place. He painted them as he saw them, without comment. Were they sometimes ugly? To him, never. "Always and everywhere," he once said to Yvette Guilbert, "ugliness has its good sides; it is exciting to discover them where no one else has noticed them before."

The people Lautrec painted were infinitely complex

Lautrec and a lovely young model, sitting in a Paris garden in 1890, a decade before his death.

and human. Each is himself and each is universal. Under his passionate brush all of them move, think, and feel. Given different clothes and hairdos, they could just as well belong to today.

So could the man who created them. To think of *la belle époque* is to conjure up a picture of the small figure walking the steep alleys of Montmartre, resting his chin on the railing in a museum, hoisting himself into an armchair. But to think of Toulouse-Lautrec, the painter, is to turn the century with him and transcend the boundaries of time.

Bibliography

Adhémar, Jean, and Jourdain, Francis, *Toulouse-Lautrec*. Paris: Editions Pierre Tisné, 1952.

Bouret, Jean, *Toulouse-Lautrec*, translated by Daphne Woodward. London: Thames and Hudson, 1964.

Céleyran, Marie Tapié de, Countess Attems, *Notre Oncle Lautrec*. Geneva: Pierre Cailler, 1963.

Fermigier, André, *Toulouse-Lautrec*, translated by Paul Stevenson. New York: Frederick A. Praeger, Inc., 1969.

Gauzi, François, *Lautrec et Son Temps*. Paris: David Perret et Cie., 1954.

Goldschmidt, Lucien, and Schimmel, Herbert, *Unpublished Correspondence of Henri de Toulouse-Lautrec*. London: Phaidon Press, Ltd., and New York: Frederick A. Praeger, Inc., 1969.

Huisman, P., and Dortu, M. G., *Lautrec par Lautrec*. Paris: Edita Lausanne, 1964.

Keller, Horst, *Toulouse-Lautrec, Painter of Paris*. New York: Harry N. Abrams, Inc., 1968.

Lassaigne, Jacques, *Toulouse-Lautrec e la Parigi dei Cabarets*. Milan: Fratelli Fabbri Editori, 1967.

Mac Orlan, Pierre, *Lautrec le Peintre*. Paris: Librairie Floury, 1934.

Mesplé, Paul, *Albi*. Paris: Les Editions du Temps, 1963.

Natanson, Thadée, *Un Henri de Toulouse-Lautrec*. Geneva: Pierre Cailler, 1961.

Perruchot, Henri, *La Vie de Toulouse-Lautrec*. Paris: Librairie Hachette, 1958.

Roger-Marx, Claude, *Yvette Guilbert Vue par Toulouse-Lautrec*. Paris: Au Pont des Arts, 1950.

Roman, Jean, *Paris Fin de Siècle*. Paris: Robert Delpire, 1958.

Cent Ans d'Affiches: "*La Belle Epoque*." Paris: Bibliothèque des Arts Décoratifs, 1964.

Catalog of the Musée Toulouse-Lautrec, Palais de la Berbie: Albi, 1967.

Catalog of the Toulouse-Lautrec Exposition at the Orangerie des Tuileries, Louvre: Paris, 1951.

Index